Your Personal Fiction-Writing Coach

Your Personal Fiction-Writing Coach

Stephanie Bond

Read this first.

So you want to be a writer? Or maybe you're already a writer, but can't seem to get that novel written? Or you've written a few books, but the thrill is gone. Is there a trick, you wonder, to writing a great book, or even finishing a so-so book? Why, yes—there are *three* tricks, actually, that veteran writers like me keep top secret (*shhhh!*):

1. Get started already.
2. Clunk through it.
3. Find ways not to stop until you get to The End.

The list probably isn't the romantic, idealistic answer you were hoping for, but I wrote this book to share with you helpful, *practical* writing advice from my twenty years as a working novelist. If you commit to reading the 365 pieces of advice that follow and (here's the important part) **write one manuscript page every day for 365 days**, then *voila!* at the end of one year, you'll have a full-length fiction manuscript of about 90,000 words.

I wrote this book with the idea of dispensing daily inspiration to get you to think about your story—and to *write*. Because I know from experience your motivation will give out before your imagination will.

This book is structured to ease you through the lifecycle of creating a full-length novel, from broad stroke advice and self-evaluating questions, to more specific tips when you get to the planning and writing stages. I've also included pitfalls to avoid, lessons I've learned and techniques to help you manage your writing time.

Can you read ahead? Sure. Skip around? Yes. Ignore one piece of advice in favor of another? Absolutely. Some of the tips will feel organic to you and your project, and some won't. You might even decide to read the entire book in one sitting—that's fine. But if you do, please commit to re-reading the book and writing one manuscript page for every section. Because I'd like for you to prove to yourself you can write a novel. Or finish the one you started. Or meet your deadline. Or rediscover the joy in writing. Or reach whatever writing goal you've set for yourself.

I see you out there, already putting on the brakes, raising your hand, bursting with questions.

"But what am I supposed to write about?"
"What does a manuscript page look like?"
"How do I get started?"
"What kind of equipment do I need?"
"What if I'm stuck?"
"What if I fail?"

Luckily for you, I have the answers to your burning questions:

Write about anything, as long as it's not boring.
A manuscript page looks like a page in a book, but with more whitespace.
To get started writing, pick up a pen, or place your hands on a keyboard.
The equipment you need to write is A) a quill and ink, or B) pen and paper, or C) a computer. (I vote "C.")
If you're stuck in your story, then something is wrong with your plot or your characters; figure it out (I'll help you) and keep going.
You will fail, absolutely, at some point. But hopefully you'll regroup and try again!

In other words, *don't go making this writing thing harder than it has to be*. Writers do that—we obsess, fret, wring our hands, drum our fingers, stare at the ceiling, sigh, delay, postpone, procrastinate, create our own obstacles, and quit before we even start, as if writing a novel is a life or death proposition. It isn't. In the scheme of things, there are much more important events going on in the world, so get over yourself a little. With some perspective, you can bring the mentally monumental task of writing a novel back down to a manageable size. After all, reading and writing aren't exactly basic human needs. And unless the book you write is a survivalist guide or medical how-to, it's probably not going to save someone's life. . . .

But it might save someone's soul. Or make them laugh. Or prompt them to read into the wee hours of the morning to find out who committed the crime, got the girl, or saved the world.

If you like guarantees, writing isn't for you. That said, if you write a novel and put it out into the universe, I *guarantee* you will:

- Learn a lot about yourself along the way. (Are you funny? Mean? Truthful? Brave?)
- Be fulfilled in a way only other writers can comprehend. (It's intoxicating.)
- Change the world some. (Something that wasn't there before, suddenly will be.)

And that's cool. Ready? Let's do this.

HEAD GAMES

So much of everything we do and don't do in life has to
do with the story we tell ourselves every day.

1. You, a novelist?

Who do you think you are, trying to write a novel? Novels are written by people who have lofty degrees and sit around in leather chairs wearing smoking jackets. Or who lounge on flowered chaises, dictating to long-suffering assistants. Novels are written by people who have something important to say, and who use a lot of big words to say it. Novels are written by people who are worldly, rich, and well-connected.

Not true, any of it. Novels are written by people in all walks of life, from all backgrounds and socioeconomic circumstances, and at all ages. Some novelists don't have anything more to say than, "Here's a good story—I hope you find it entertaining." The beautiful part is, that's good enough. Because all a reader wants is to pass a few hours being transported from their situation to the one you're offering.

2. Requirements for being a novelist

If you have a college degree in English or creative writing or journalism, then good for you—you're a little ahead of the rest of us. But you don't need a degree in any of those fields, or a degree at all, to be a novelist. The only requirements for being a novelist are:

- You're a dedicated reader, meaning you love to read and books are important to you.
- You're a prolific reader—you've read a little bit of everything, and a lot in the genre you most enjoy.
- You have a basic knowledge of story structure (beginning, middle, end), which you've probably absorbed from years of reading without thinking about it.
- You have access to basic computer equipment to produce a manuscript: a laptop or other type of input device, and word processing software.
- You have time to dedicate to your writing.
- You're self-motivated. Because there will be countless reasons to give up all along the way. Every day. At. Every. Turn.

At this point, the primary difference between you and a published novelist is they finished writing their book.

3. Why do you want to be a writer?

The answer to the question above seems obvious—because you want to write! But what do you want to accomplish with your writing? Do you want to entertain? Explain an idea or situation? Persuade readers to join a cause or change their mind about something? Further your own personal platform? Do you want to be a hobby writer who documents a family tree or stories passed down through generations? Maybe you're writing for yourself, for therapy, or just to prove to your own satisfaction you can write a novel. Or is your goal publication with the idea of earning money for your effort, perhaps even to leave your current job and become a self-supporting full-time writer?

All of these motives are admirable, but require different levels of commitment and will take you down different paths. This is a good time to ask yourself what your own expectations are. Ultimately, you're the person you have to impress.

4. What will everyone think of you?

If people find out you're writing a book, what will they think? That you've lost your mind? That you're going to spill a family secret, or put them in your book? That you'll write something salacious that will embarrass them? Maybe your spouse is supportive, but what about your minister, your neighbors, your coworkers, your children's teachers, or *gulp*—your mother?

Okay, so here's the thing: As a writer, you must come to terms with the material you're writing and decide if you want to consider how it might affect the people in your life. They *will* read it—at least the first book. And it's true some people will not be able to separate what they read from the writer. If you write about serial killers, drug addiction, kinky sex, infidelity, or international espionage, they might assume you're writing from experience. And hey, maybe you are! But probably not. Writing under a pseudonym will help to hide your identity to a certain degree, but not entirely. Let me assure you most writers have a few qualms about people close to them reading their work and judging them, but we get over it relatively quickly. Still, consider your privacy (or lack of) as you plan what you're going to write.

5. The state of the book industry

I'm not sure any industry has changed as radically as the book industry in the last ten years. Technology has changed every aspect of the business from creation to distribution to purchasing to consumption. Print books haven't died the quick death predicted, but eBooks have permanently altered the course of bookselling. Even if you're a luddite, you need to understand your audience might be consuming your end-product on a phone, tablet, or dedicated e-reader. And some genres lend themselves to digital reading more than others.

In general, the younger and the more male your audience, the more likely they will be reading your book electronically. Ditto if the genre is wildly popular (like romance) because the more prolific the reader, the more likely he/she is loading up their e-reader versus accumulating physical inventory. (It's not uncommon for romance readers to read a book a day.) But it's all good news for writers because reading is sexy again! Books are viral. Characters have their own social media accounts. Stories are in demand, no matter the format.

If you're serious about becoming a writer, you should set aside a few hours and read recent articles about the state of the book industry just to be aware of what's going on, what's selling, what's not selling, and how readers' habits are affected by technology.

6. Why you probably should quit now

Truthful writers will tell you being a writer is akin to standing naked on a pedestal in bad lighting in the middle of a train station and letting every passerby give their opinion. (This analogy is more harrowing when you realize most writers spend a lot of time sitting, not so much time in the gym.) So you will spend untold hours writing your novel, alienating friends and family in the process and putting a crimp in your back. And when you finally release your novel into the universe, it might not be read by as many people as you hope. And the ones who read it might not like it. Worse—their reviews are right there for everyone to see, including the ex who said you'd never amount to anything. And even if your book is well-received, only a small percentage of writers earn enough money to live on. So if you're a rational being, you probably should quit now, while the quitting is good.

But you won't quit, will you? Because the magical mystique of storytelling calls to you, and you know you have something to say, something that's never been said before, and won't ever be said if you don't put it out there. And that makes you special. Because you dare to do something even when the odds of succeeding are stacked against you. Hm…sounds like the makings of a good story, doesn't it?

7. It's competitive out there

All it takes is one visit to a bookstore or a quick browsing session at an online retailer to realize how competitive the book business has become. Historically, lots of new books are released every month, but now that electronic books are available, a book rarely goes "out of print," so the accumulation of inventory continues...and will continue to continue. It's easy to feel overwhelmed at the thought of breaking in with a new book among millions of other titles. But instead of focusing on the number of books and the big-named authors you'll have to compete with, think instead that all those people wrote a book, and you can, too!

8. The road is long...

That phrase is the beginning of a classic song performed by The Hollies, and the description of the journey every writer embarks upon. There's a lot to learn...you have a lot to say...and there are countless ways to say it. You're going to spend a great deal of precious time writing your novel. After the book is written, if your goal is to be published by a traditional publisher, you will spend a lot more time submitting your work for consideration and staring at your phone or inbox waiting for someone to say "Yes." And after yes, still more time waiting for the book to debut. Even if you decide to self-publish, the lifecycle of a book is long—you might not receive the instant and positive response you're dreaming of.

A private investigator once told me she spent most of her time sitting and watching and waiting for someone else to do something. Not unlike the writing profession!

This journey will test your patience, your pride, and your peace of mind. But it'll be worth it. You'll see.

9. What's a genre, and how do you get one?

If it's been a while since you've been to a bookstore, now's the time for a little field trip. To write a sell-able book, you sort of need to write something that will fit into a category, and it's best to know what categories readers identify with. A category is also known as a *genre*. For fiction, a genre might be romance or mystery or science fiction or literary fiction, and might be further classified by age group—young adult literary fiction, for example. You can also go to an online bookstore and look at the categories offered to readers. If you're not sure what your targeted genre is, find a book you've read that most closely mirrors what you want to write and see how it's categorized.

Note that some categories overlap—romantic suspense, for example. (In this case, "romantic suspense" is a sub-genre of romance.) I categorize some of my novels as "romantic mysteries" because they're a blend of two genres. When I wrote for traditional publishers and brick-and-mortar bookstores were the main sales outlets, blending genres was a problem because the books weren't easily shelved in one section of a store. Different bookstore chains shelved my novels in different sections—it was confusing to readers. Now that most sales are through online bookstores, it's much easier to sell a hybrid genre book because it can be tagged with more than one category.

10. Writer, read!

Once you identify your genre, read widely within it. I'm amazed at the people I meet who want to write a romance novel, but when I ask a few questions, it's clear they're not familiar with the elements of the genre. I recommend you read at least fifty books in your chosen genre, both bestsellers and obscure titles. As mentioned before, you'll discover every genre can be further divided—the mystery genre, for instance, can be subdivided into cozy, police procedural, amateur sleuth, etc. The more thoroughly you know your genre, the better your chance of writing a book that will be accepted by an established group of readers.

If you're thinking, *My book can't be categorized,* you're in trouble. If no book exists that's similar to yours, that's a big red flag. Don't try to slay that dragon on your first book—write something that will appeal to an established group of readers, but make the story your own.

11. Should you write what you read?

Maybe. It's true you probably gravitate toward writing in a particular genre because you've always read in that genre. But I encourage you to explore beyond the borders of your typical reading selections to make sure you're not unwittingly excluding an area in which you might excel. For example, the first book-length manuscript I started writing was a historical romance because it's what I most loved to read. But I was writing in my spare time around a full-time job, and I was getting so bogged down in research, I was afraid I'd never finish writing the manuscript. So, I switched to writing contemporary romance, specifically family drama—emotional, heart-wrenching stories.

It wasn't until an editor read a cover letter I'd written for a workshop and commented on my "humorous voice" that a light came on for me. I'm not a funny person—I don't tell jokes well, and I don't always get the punchline when other people tell them. But for some reason, what I don't express in person comes out in my writing. From that moment on, I turned my attention to writing comedy. The first manuscript I sold was a romantic comedy to Harlequin Enterprises titled *Irresistible?* And with only a couple of exceptions, my books since then have featured a comedic tone. With this in mind, don't assume your talents lie in the genre or sub-genre you've been reading. The possibilities are varied and waiting to be discovered!

12. Experiment

If you're at an early stage of your writing career, I suggest you experiment with writing in different genres (romance, mystery, science fiction, fantasy, general fiction, historical fiction, etc.) and in different lengths (short stories, novellas, full-length novels) to get a feel for all the avenues open to you. Subscribing to writing magazines will expose you to different genres and formats. When I first started writing, I wrote short stories because I (wrongly) assumed they were easier. I also wrote a column for a sewing magazine, and a business column for my local writing chapter newsletter. Every word helped to shape and refine my writing style. Remember, *writing begets writing*.

13. Genre-hop at your own risk

When you find a good genre fit and you know in your bones it's what you want to write, it's time to stop experimenting and focus your efforts in one area. The most successful writers confine their efforts to one genre (or subgenre); doing so helps readers to find and keep finding your books.

But writers are creatives, and creatives want to do what they want to do, so it's not uncommon for authors to genre-hop whenever the mood strikes them or they get bored. (Genre-hopping isn't the same as blending genres into one book, which readers are more accepting of, especially if you keep doing it.) While writing a completely different kind of book the next time around might offer instant gratification for you, it can confuse and frustrate your readers who buy your subsequent books expecting them to be similar to the earlier ones. Some writers cue readers to their different types of books by using a different pen name…but then they're splintering their marketing efforts across two or more pen names. Why make it so hard on yourself?

In my opinion, the most efficient way to build a readership is to accumulate a consistent body of work in one genre or sub-genre under one name.

14. Commercial fiction vs. literary fiction

This one seems to stump new writers, but there is a difference between commercial fiction and literary fiction. Commercial fiction is typically what comes to mind when you think of big blockbuster bestsellers. Commercial fiction usually encompasses thrillers or mysteries or romances or science fiction novels. They are pure entertainment. Literary fiction, on the other hand, is generally thought of as books with a message, perhaps with a more obscure subject matter, and told with a more lyrical or experimental writing style. Often referred to as "book club books," literary fiction doesn't always deliver the happy ending of commercial fiction. With a literary novel, the reader might instead get a "satisfying" ending, or one that's thought-provoking. One way to distinguish commercial fiction from literary fiction is to think of it this way: Commercial fiction raises questions, then answers them for the reader; literary fiction raises questions, then leaves the answers for the reader to decide.

So when you think of the type of book you want to write, would you categorize it as commercial fiction or literary fiction?

15. What is voice?

After I sold my first manuscript, I asked my editor if she expected me to take writing classes or get an MFA in creative writing. Her response was, "No! Don't take any classes—it will ruin your voice!"

At the time I had a vague idea of what "voice" meant, and since then have learned more. A writer's voice is much like an individual's speaking voice—it's unique. A speaking voice is made up of lots of different elements: tone, pitch, grammar, word choice, how well a person projects, their accent, their cadence, subject matter, etc.

Similarly, a writer's voice is what sets their writing apart from everyone else's and is made up of many things: grammar, word choice, tone, cadence, subject matter, etc. Your writing voice is your writing fingerprint and your competitive edge. Establishing a distinct voice is the single most important skill you can develop as a writer. How can you do that?

It's difficult to identify your own writing voice because it's so inherent. Consider instead working with a critique partner to help each other pinpoint your individual voices, i.e., where your talent as a writer really sparkles. You might have a comedic voice, a suspenseful voice, a gift for description and atmosphere, or a flair for dialogue. Or perhaps you tell a certain kind of story (southern family sagas, political thrillers) with ringing authenticity. Once you identify your writing voice, let it sing.

16. What should you write about?

One thing that paralyzes aspiring (and veteran) novelists is the big question of what to write about. When you can write about anything in the universe, it's easy to get lost in the sheer enormity of choices. The pressure can and does shut down some writers before they even get started.

Remember this charge: As a writer, *your primary job is to make decisions.* To start narrowing down topics, you must accept the fact that by saying yes to one idea, you're saying no to other ideas that might be just as compelling. That's okay—by choosing an idea, you're not saying this is the best and brightest and most important idea you will ever think of—you're simply saying *this* is the idea you're going to tackle in *this* manuscript. Those other ideas will still be waiting for you when you're ready to write another project.

WARMUP

Increase your chances of success by getting yourself
mentally and physically prepared for the task ahead!

17. How to get started

One of the best ways to come up with a book idea is simply to brainstorm "What if" questions: What if a woman met the child she gave up for adoption on a train? What if one day the sun didn't come up? What if the guy in the mailroom discovered he has super powers?

Another exercise I use to jumpstart my imagination is to picture a scene and challenge myself to come up with at least ten ways to explain it. For example, the scene is a woman cutting her own hair. Why?

1. She's broke and can't afford to go to a salon.
2. She's giving herself a makeover for a date.
3. She's donating her hair to charity.
4. She's trying to disguise her identity.
5. She just awoke from a coma that lasted long enough for her hair to grow out.
6.
7.
8.
9.
10.

Get the idea? The longer the list, the more creative the excuse, and the more story ideas come to mind. Try it! Can you think of five more reasons a woman would be cutting her own hair?

18. Managing ideas

Before my smart phone, I always kept paper and pen on me in case a brilliant idea popped into my head when I was away from my laptop. (I confess, however, that I've been known to write on napkins, receipts, and gum wrappers. My drycleaner knows to check the pockets of my clothing.) Later I transfer the ideas to a file on my computer aptly titled IDEAS. I suggest you create one, too. This will be the place where you can record snippets and snatches of ideas, half-baked or full-blown, until you're ready to call them to duty. You can also drop in pictures or links to research articles. Not only have I consulted the file countless times to find fresh story ideas, but if I felt the manuscript I was writing needed a subplot or something extra, my IDEAS file was my salvation.

19. There is no such thing as an original idea

Now that you're busily storing away ideas for your novel like a squirrel gathering nuts for the winter, I'm going to touch on a subject that almost always comes up among writers: *How can I keep someone from stealing my idea?*

The short answer is, you can't—ideas aren't copyrightable. But the long answer is even if you learn someone is writing a story similar to the one you're working on, you shouldn't assume they stole it from you, nor should you abandon the idea. The truth is, sometimes ideas are simply "in the air" and two or more writers have the same idea at the same time. Maybe something in the news or a popular song sparks a similar idea. Or maybe a cultural trend or a catchy phrase triggers a concept. There really is no such thing as an original idea anyway—all the basic plots have been done thousands of times. But the spin you put on an old plot is what makes it fresh and original.

Early in my career I wrote a book titled *Our Husband* about three women who discover they're all married to the same man. The same month my book was released, a historical romance author released a book about three women who travel to the West to find the man they learn they're all married to. I knew of the author, but we weren't acquaintances. Still, I remember lots of reviewers accusing me of stealing her idea, or vice versa. Which is ridiculous when you consider how long it takes to get a book in and out of the publishing pipeline. It was simply a matter of synchronicity.

20. What is high concept?

A high concept idea, in my opinion, can be one of two things:

1) An idea with universal appeal (tried and true), but with a contemporary twist
2) An idea global in scope and consequences (cinematic)

For example:

Universal appeal (tried and true): a parent who has lost a child
Contemporary twist: told from the murdered child's point of view
Book: *The Lovely Bones* by Alice Sebold

Global in scope and consequences (cinematic): A professor stumbles onto the secret that Jesus Christ may have produced a child.
Book: *The Da Vinci Code* by Dan Brown

Using some of my own books for further examples (all of which fall in the first category):

Universal appeal (tried and true): A working girl struggles with life issues
Contemporary twist: She works for Neiman Marcus by day and moves bodies from crime scenes by night.
Book: *Body Movers*

Universal appeal (tried and true): A woman is recovering from a messy divorce

Contemporary twist: She stabs a voodoo doll of her ex as a joke, and he's found murdered.
Book: *In Deep Voodoo*

Movie people in particular are fond of the "high concept" expressed in a pithy logline that would look good on a movie poster. Remember, a high concept idea can be expressed with a minimum of words, i.e., everyone "gets it" without a lot of explanation.

21. What to do with small ideas

If you have an idea, but it's not exactly high concept, can you still use it to write a novel? You can—think of the TV show *Seinfeld* that was billed as a situation comedy about nothing, yet every episode was relatable because each one featured small things we all deal with in our own lives. A book with a small idea (plot) is typically more of a character-driven novel. And if you make your character vivid enough, you can get away with the character doing something less grand than say, becoming an FBI informant. Just know that a character-driven novel is more challenging to write because you don't have big plot points to "hang" your story on.

If you have a small idea, you might consider writing a short story or novella, or incorporating it as a subplot into a bigger book. Or you could start with a small idea—your character is frustrated by his neighbor's barking dog, for example—and see where it leads:

> *A man is jarred awake by a barking dog in the apartment next to his. He bangs on the wall to quieten the dog and a chunk of the wall collapses, exposing a duffel bag...*

So there really is no such thing as a small idea.

22. Too many ideas in one book

I have a writing friend who is clever and prolific and enthusiastic about writing. She should be a household name. But she's had difficulty selling her books because she tends to clobber the reader with too many plot lines in one book:

Her hero is not just an FBI agent, he's a vampire. And he's a vampire because many centuries ago in another land, he was pursuing a serial killer, who turned out to be himself, because he has multiple personalities, and when he realized he was a murderer he persuaded a local vampire to bite him so he could have everlasting life on earth to right his wrongs…which is kind of backfiring on him because he has to kill people to stay alive. But when he meets the heroine, everything changes. The heroine is not just an innocent, she's a nun. And she's the great-great granddaughter of a woman the vampire murdered back when he was just a plain old human serial killer. And…

Is your head hurting yet? Right. My friend is a great storyteller, but she puts so many plot lines and so much backstory into her books, they get muddy and complicated. She gets bogged down in too many details and loses sight of moving the plot forward.

If you have too many ideas in your book, chip away the extraneous detail until you get down to one solid high concept idea. The book will be easier to write, easier to sell, and easier to read.

23. "So, what's your book about?"

Inevitably, when people know you're writing a novel, they will ask, "So, what's your book about?" The very question spikes your adrenaline—nothing is quite as exciting as talking about the novel you're writing. That said, you should know despite their polite question, the person asking does not want a thirty-minute description of the plot, characters, setting, and backstory. Nor do they want a fifteen-minute description. Truth be told, they don't even want a five-minute description—all they want is the setup. Before you get your feelings hurt, you should view the opening as an opportunity to hone your pitch. Your pitch of the setup is one or two sentences, max.

"*Body Movers* is about a woman who works at Neiman Marcus by day and helps her brother move bodies from crime scenes by night." *Boom*. That's enough. I could add their parents have been missing for a decade. I could add the brother is in debt to loan sharks up to his eyeballs. I could add the sister's first love who dumped her over her parents' scandal is back in her life. I could add a dozen different details that add to the complexity of the story, but they're not necessary to understand *what my book is about*.

Try to distill the setup of your book into one or two sentences. You'll be ready when someone asks—and you will dazzle them with your brevity.

24. Imagination drill!

A man in a coffee shop gets a call on his phone, talks briefly, then hangs up and gives a fist pump in the air. What was his news? Can you come up with 10 ideas that run the gamut from happy to sinister?

1.

2.

3.

4.

5.

6.

7.

8.

9.

10.

(For printable PDFs of all Imagination Drills, go to
www.stephaniebond.com.)

25. Plotting your novel

In the previous section, I talked about the setup of your book. But the plot of your book is so much more—the plot starts with the setup, but then this happens, and that happens, then THAT happens, etc., etc., and the story snowballs to a climax, then you tie up all the loose ends. Think of your plot as a curtain rod and your story as a curtain. The plot is what everything else hangs on. It has to be strong and in my opinion, should be well-thought-out before you begin writing. The general purpose of the plot is to keep your story moving forward. Here's a basic story plot:

- We meet the main character. We see them in their normal "world."
- An inciting incident introduces a problem and takes the main character out of their world.
- The main character is propelled forward to another situation, which triggers something else, and so on.
- Along the way, the main character encounters other characters who either help or complicate the situation.
- Things go in one direction for a while, then are pulled in another direction.
- The situation builds and then suddenly, it looks as if things are going to work out (Plateau of Happiness).
- But then everything gets even worse!
- The situation builds to a stormy climax (Black Moment).
- The problem is resolved.

- The main character's world has somehow changed; even if it looks the same, the main character sees their world through a new lens.

Sound too simple? Take any movie, book, or TV show and overlay the story on the above structure and you'll see it's pretty universal.

26. Inciting incident

One mistake new *and* veteran authors make is neglecting to explain the catalyst of the story, the reason *why* the character is suddenly behaving the way they are or the reason the story is taking place *now*. *Why* did your heroine wake up this morning and decide to divorce her husband/quit her job/adopt a child? It's more vivid and concrete for the reader if you provide a catalyst for the action that's about to be undertaken, and it's best to show the scene— a milestone birthday party? Being passed over for a promotion? A pregnancy scare? A catalyst means change, and change is always interesting.

27. The Plateau of Happiness

This is the point in the story where readers (and your character) get a glimmer of how good things can be. For a while, it looks as if things are going to work out—everyone is feeling good. But good = boring, so the Plateau of Happiness should be very short. Ten minutes, maybe. Picture the Plateau of Happiness as the characters happily walking along having conquered something and thinking their problems are over. They're slapping each other on the back or holding hands...and then they fall off a cliff.

28. The Black Moment

The most successful movies and books are those where the reader/viewer can scan the back cover copy or watch the trailer and instantly anticipate the Black Moment. The Black Moment is when all the problems in your story reach their pinnacle, when the hero/heroine is confronted with their worst fear/greatest challenge and all seems lost: they are out-manned, out-gunned, seemingly out-witted, totally vulnerable, and generally looking death in the face—either figuratively, or literally.

For example, if your setup is "a man tells a lie in order to secure a job he desperately needs to keep his family from being evicted," the Black Moment will be when his lie is discovered. If your setup doesn't inspire the anticipation of the Black Moment, you need to backtrack.

29. What's at stake?

When you're plotting your book, you should ask yourself "What's at stake?" In other words, what will happen if my character acts or doesn't act? Your story will be greatly enhanced if something is at stake, either for the main character, someone they're close to, the world at large, etc.

Stakes can range from small (if your character doesn't get out of bed on time, he/she will be late to work) to epic (if your character doesn't stop the terrorist attack, a government will fall), and can be internal (if your character doesn't know the answer to a question in class, he/she will be embarrassed), or external (if your character finds a way to cut costs, three employees won't be fired).

Internal and external stakes can work together—picture the reluctant hero who takes on a challenge because he doesn't want to look inept in front of his girlfriend...only to discover the (external) stakes are much higher than he originally thought.

Ideally, stakes should escalate in a story to create more tension and urgency. When you think about the hierarchy of stakes, it's tempting to say loss of life is the highest of stakes. But what about the life of a man versus the life of a child? Or what about a principle? Countless people have died to defend or preserve something they believe in.

When you plan your novel, make sure you convey what's at stake.

30. Throughline

One of the biggest problems I see with unpublished manuscripts is somewhere along the line, the writer loses the "throughline" of the story. (Shockingly, this also happens in more movies than I can count.) Think of your plot as a straight line, like the curtain rod I mentioned before. A good story has twists and turns, but the reader has to be able to draw a mental straight line from the beginning of the story to the end. In other words, your novel shouldn't be one kind of story in the beginning and change to another type of story before getting to the end, i.e., start as a medical thriller and wind up being a tale about angels. You can have subplots in your story, also referred to as the "B" story, the "C" story, etc., but the central issue of the story—the "A" story—shouldn't change. Don't be tempted to go off on tangents that will yank the story too far in another direction. A subplot should support and reinforce the main plot in some way, not detract from it.

31. Can you write about events
from your own life?

I believe writers can't help but draw from their own life experiences—we put a tiny bit of ourselves into every novel. If you do write about events from your own life, I suggest you embellish or tone down as necessary to make the event appropriate for the type of book you're writing. I remember reading a book written by a friend and one scene in particular seemed out of place— the pacing and the wording changed and the scene briefly interrupted the flow of storytelling. When I told my friend how much I'd enjoyed the book, she asked if I remembered a certain scene? I said I did. She laughed and said, "That actually happened to me." Which explained everything. Because when writers are determined to shoehorn their own experience into a fictional story, they can unwittingly make it too specific, too detailed and out of sync with the rest of the story. This is referred to as "author intrusion." If you draw from true events in your life when you write your novel, be mindful of not inserting yourself into the story in a way that disrupts the telling.

32. Can you write about events from someone else's life?

Exercise caution when writing about events from someone else's life that you weren't personally involved in. Unless they're a public figure, you could be exposing yourself to a lawsuit. Even if the person has given you verbal permission and even if you let them read the material before you publish it, unless you get their permission in writing, you could put yourself in jeopardy. Good feelings might swing if the person's circumstances change or if your book sells well. If you base a story on someone else's experiences, I suggest you change the name, place, and enough details so no one else will recognize the person's story. I know of circumstances where novelists have been sued by acquaintances for basing a story too closely on true events. With everything you could write about, why risk it?

33. Fan fiction

Fan fiction is fiction written in a "world" created by another writer, using elements from that world including setting, characters, and situations. Note that since a writer's characters are copyrighted, fan fiction is generally considered to be copyright infringement, and exists mostly in fan fiction forums. But that's changing. There are now opportunities for "author sanctioned" fan fiction in which an author licenses their world to a publisher who will publish fan fiction and pay the fan fiction author a royalty. Writing fan fiction is appealing to some writers because it offers a basic structure to write within, and a built-in audience.

Note that anyone can write fan fiction around a property considered public domain (in the United States, generally books published before 1923), meaning the copyright has expired, without fear of recrimination.

(If the idea of writing fan fiction intrigues you, I encourage you to check out Amazon's Kindle Worlds, an author-sanctioned program for writing fan fiction that allows you to earn royalties. To-date, I've licensed two series to Kindle Worlds, my *Body Movers* mystery series, and my *Southern Roads* romance series. And there are dozens of other Kindle Worlds to choose from, in every genre.)

34. Story elements to avoid

If you're writing your first novel, there are some topics more difficult than others to write about and sell. Match your subject matter to your experience and knowledge base. Unless you have a background in police work, tackling an FBI thriller or a police procedural will require a lot of research and finesse to write with authority. Ditto for political and medical thrillers. Can a novice pull it off? Sure. But you'll be competing with authors who have careers in those fields, so be aware the bar is high. Don't set your sights on writing an international spy adventure simply because you think you need to write something "epic" to get attention. The same can be said for topical news items—don't include issues such as child abuse and racism and terrorism simply because you think it will make your book "bigger." All plot elements should feel organic to the storyline, else those elements will seem gratuitous.

35. Story elements readers love

There are some universal story elements readers flock to. Family dysfunction is popular because it hits a nerve for almost all readers. Life events such as births, deaths, weddings, and funerals never go out of style because they're incidents readers can relate to. Turning 30, 40, 50, etc., are perennial favorite story elements, as are fish-out-of-water stories, love triangles, and reunion stories. Why? All the elements I listed are rife with emotional fallout, and readers know when emotions are high, anything can happen...and often does. If you want to engage your reader, consider including a proven story element in your overall plot.

36. Writing for a global market

More than ever before, writers are creating stories for a global market. It's worth your time to review elements of your novel and ask yourself how they might be received by someone living in another country, whose life, family, work, and travel experiences are probably much different than your own. While it's not possible to write a book every single person on the planet will love and relate to, there are some things you can do to make your plot and characters more recognizable. If you have the opportunity to set your book in any city, set it in a city people in other countries will be familiar with. And use names that aren't too complicated. Also, be careful about using idioms and slang that might be confusing to readers who don't live in the region where you set your story. And consider building a diverse cast of characters for your book, characters of varied ethnicities and backgrounds.

37. Trends

Like every consumer product, books go through trends. Usually, those trends are content related—genres and sub-genres go in and out of vogue. In the romance industry, reader demand for paranormal, historical, suspenseful, and comedic stories rise and fall every few years. The genres of glitz, erotica, chick-lit, hen-lit, and granny-lit have all created bestsellers and rabid readers...then virtually disappeared (for a while). Death and dying novels were once all the rage in young adult books, and have come back around. The "new adult" genre is an upstart book category, bolstered by the fact that people of all ages are reading young adult and new adult books. Types of characters within genres also fall in and out of favor: Within the paranormal genre, vampires give way to werewolves which give way to witches which give way to angels which give way to ghosts which give way to vampires. And in the romance genre, there's always a hero *du jour:* cowboys, millionaires, dukes, sheikhs, detectives, athletes, rock stars, geeks.

The point is, if you try to chase trends, you'll probably always be a little behind the curve, and constantly on a pivot. Try to construct your novel to have broad appeal and to be timeless in terms of content. If, however, you are in love with a trendy element (meaning, it's not a trend to you), know you'll always have an audience, but the audience might shrink and swell as readers' tastes change.

38. Your main character

Your main character is arguably the most important aspect of your book. This is the person you have to persuade your reader to believe in, root for, care about, or be fascinated by. Your reader has to be invested in your main character and feel empathy for him/her. In order to convince your reader your main character is a living, breathing person, he/she must first be real to you. It's important to give your main character a background that explains who they've become as a person. Keep in mind the reader doesn't have to know every detail you've created for your main character—this exercise is for you and your character to bond and connect in a way that makes you eager to write about him/her for a few hundred pages. If you aren't riveted by your main character, how can you expect your reader to be?

39. Character vocation

How your main character makes a living (or doesn't) says a lot about them. Do they live in a place where they can make a decision about their vocation, or do they live in a time/place where social/governmental pressures force them down a certain path? Is your main character educated? Did they get an education in one field and are now working in another field? Is their job quirky, or predictable? Does it pay well? How do they feel about their employment situation? How has it affected other aspects of their life?

But it's not simply enough to assign your character a random job title— ideally their occupation should have something to do with the plot of the story. Additionally, the chosen occupation should highlight the character's strengths *and* their weaknesses.

If you're stumped for a vocation for a character, there are good sources online. Most astrology sites suggest vocations by a person's sign/personality. Or check out the classifieds in your local newspaper or job sites online—the ads will usually describe what kind of person they're looking for in terms of qualities and education.

By the way, if your character is heir to a family fortune and doesn't have to work, or lives on the street and chooses not to work, those circumstances define them, too.

40. Character growth

Okay, this one's a biggie, so bookmark it, highlight it, turn down the corner of the page or whatever you have to do to mark its importance. The number one mistake writers at all levels make is *not ensuring the main character experiences emotional growth by the end of the story.*

In the attempt to feature a character who is likable, relatable, and heroic, you can inadvertently create a character who is too perfect. Instead, you should strive to present someone who is likable, relatable, and heroic, but also has idiosyncrasies, quirks, phobias, compulsions, and flaws. In other words, you need to give your character room to face a foible, become a better person, or learn a lesson. You need to start him/her in a slightly broken place.

That said, in some genres—romance, for example—there are certain flaws that go too far and speak to the soul of a character. Your hero should never strike the heroine or make unwelcome or threatening sexual advances. Likewise, your heroine should never manipulate the hero by doing something abominable such as faking a pregnancy. Yes, your characters have their problems and idiosyncrasies, but they are noble. Their worst sins should be against themselves, not against other people. And if they do something to hurt another person, they should go to great measures to remedy the situation.

41. Cast of characters

When I build a supporting cast of characters for the hero and heroine, I call the process "rubberizing" the characters because I'm trying to create characters who will bounce off each other. Secondary characters are the most beneficial to your story when they highlight the main characters by being a perfect foil—if your heroine is a bit kooky, her best friend might be deadpan. If the hero is a neat freak, his coworker might be a slob.

Every secondary character should have a distinct role in furthering the plot, but ideally, should be tied into the story through a main character. While it's possible for a secondary character to have their own story unfold in a subplot, make sure the stories are closely tied together.

For instance, let's say your book is about a woman who is looking into the unexplained death of her father. Her estranged sister is introduced as a secondary character. Then the sister is arrested for a crime, and the heroine has to come to her aid. Ideally, the crime the sister is arrested for should somehow tie back to the main plot of the unexplained death of the father. In other words, it's best if all the story threads eventually tie together.

A secondary character is also a good choice to demonstrate how close to danger the hero or heroine is—they're a likely target for villains to show they're closing in on their real target, the main character. A secondary character might also be a way for the main character to experience something vicariously. For instance, if the heroine is contemplating marriage, helping her sister plan her wedding might make the heroine rethink her own goals.

42. Secondary characters who endure

Can you think of a book, movie, or TV show where a secondary character became a fan favorite? When creating secondary characters, you want them to support and highlight the main character, but be able to step into the spotlight if necessary. With that in mind, beware of falling back on stereotypes; secondary characters have to seem as real to the reader as the main characters, and stereotypical characters seem more cartoonish than real. This is especially true when creating characters of a race and culture different than your own. One-dimensional secondary characters will only detract from your story.

Just be careful your secondary character doesn't take over, which can happen when you write a quirky character who's more "fun" to write than the main character, who might be more strait-laced by comparison. Secondary characters are there to add flavor; don't let them steal every scene.

43. Character names

Putting some thought into naming a character is important because it helps you to build the right tone for your character—sweet, hard-edged, down-to-earth, arrogant, a regular Joe, a princess, or even a killer. Consider how the following classic character names lent to their characterization: Scarlett O'Hara, Clark Kent, Hannibal Lecter.

Character names that are short and heavy with hard consonants suggest a character is strong: Jake, Kate, Dirk, Luke, Pete, Brooke. Conversely, longer character names with lots of vowels seem softer to the eye and ear: Angelina, Evangeline, Aaron, Isadora.

If your character has an unusual personality, it helps to tag them with a distinctive name readers will remember: Tuesday, Ivory, Zelda, Griffin. For proof a name helps to form personality, look to celebrity parents who give their children one-of-a-kind names like Apple and Suri and North—it's a good bet they're trying to stamp their children with individuality from the onset.

And remember the character's full name is important—make sure the surname you choose "goes with" the first name. And some characters are just begging for a middle name (Bobbi Ann Callihan), or a family title (Douglas Bartholomew Holloway, Jr.). Look for a certain flow to help establish your character as someone who has "grown into" their name, whether it be confining or unrestrained.

44. Characterization exercises

I'm going to really pester you about getting to know your characters so you can find out if they can pull off the plot you have planned. It's better to know now if they need to be tweaked.

One way to find out more about your characters is to interview them—pose questions such as "What was your childhood like?" and "What's the worst thing that ever happened to you?"

Another exercise is to make a list of the things your hero would have in his wallet, or your heroine would have in her purse.

And another way to determine what's most important to your characters is to list the one thing they would go back for if their home was on fire?

As your story progresses, you'll want to drop in those juicy details about your characters to make them more three-dimensional and more memorable.

45. The anti-hero

Lately in movies and TV shows, the anti-hero has become popular. The anti-hero is often the reluctant hero, perhaps curmudgeonly and unpleasant, even arrogant. His appeal is in his knowledge-base and expertise—he always has the right answer, even if he delivers it bluntly and with little respect for anyone's feelings. He shows just enough glimpses of humanity to be tolerable and just when you think he's soul-less, he does something redeemable. The anti-hero fosters his sour persona because something in his background keeps him from connecting with others; his gruff demeanor is a way to keep people at arm's length. Alternately, some phobia or physical limitation keeps him from having relationships with people, even if he wants to. Secretly, he's lonely.

All of the above could apply to an anti-heroine, too! Consider Scarlett O'Hara in Margaret Mitchell's classic *Gone With the Wind*.

46. Can you use real people in your story?

In an earlier segment, I discussed the risks of basing a story on something that happened to an acquaintance. But you might be wondering if you can include real people in your stories, i.e., mention them by name. Including real people is only permissible if the person has a "public persona," meaning some notoriety that makes their name recognizable to readers. Celebrities, politicians, and some figures in the news are considered to have a public persona. That said, if you mention a real person's name in your story, you should try to do it in a positive or neutral way, just to be safe.

47. Faction

In recent years, a new genre of fiction has emerged called "faction." Faction is fiction set in an authentic historical period, featuring cameos of famous people who lived during the time, with inventions, discoveries, and head-lines of the day woven into the story. Faction blends the truth-telling of history and the fabrication of fiction, and the story possibilities are endless. You have more leeway when you feature in your story a person has been deceased for a long time, but in my opinion, if you attribute something fictional to that person, you should let readers know.

48. Animals as characters

Readers love animals, so if you feel inclined to please, you might consider including furred, finned, or feathered characters in your story. Pets add to their masters' characterization, and can provide comic relief. Animals can also add to a story's atmosphere: Consider the spooky connotation of wolves, crows, snakes, roaches, and alternately, the inspirational connotation of puppies, horses, doves, and butterflies.

In my book *Kill the Competition*, the heroine inherited a cat from a man who'd left her at the altar. She and the cat didn't like each other, but they'd both been dumped and eventually bonded. In other books I've featured a rescue dog (*Baby, Hold On*), a finicky python (*Body Movers* series), a mouthy parrot (*Club Cupid*) and even a pet deer (*Southern Roads* series).

A little aside here: Unless your animal is a vampire, werewolf, werecat, or other shapeshifter, please don't give them a point of view and dialogue. I'm just saying.

49. Which is more important, plot or character?

If you want to start an argument, ask a group of writers which is more important—plot or character. Here's my take: When it comes to *writing* a good book, character is more important. If you make your character interesting enough, you can get away with less plot because the reader is willing to follow along no matter what your character does or doesn't do. But when it comes to *selling* a book, you need plot. It's difficult to convey characterization in a cover letter...and in back cover copy. So the best of both worlds is to create a compelling character, and give them something interesting to do.

50. Imagination drill!

A child is hiding in a locker at school. Can you think of 10 explanations ranging from funny to spine-tingling?

1.

2.

3.

4.

5.

6.

7.

8.

9.

10.

(For printable PDFs of all Imagination Drills, go to
www.stephaniebond.com.)

51. Conflict

Every story is about conflict—your character wants *this*, but the entity (person, organization, army) they're forced to interact with wants *that*:

- Your heroine wants to remain single, but her boyfriend wants to get married.
- Your hero wants a raise, but his boss has someone else in mind.
- Your retired hero wants to go fishing, but a crisis that requires his expertise interrupts his vacation.
- Your heroine wants to find the buried treasure, but so does the person who actually has the map.

Conflict is simply another word for "problem." And your story needs a problem—lots of them. Here's what happens when there's no problem:

- Your heroine wants to remain single, and so does her boyfriend. THE END
- Your hero wants a raise, and his boss agrees. THE END
- Your retired hero wants to go fishing, and he does. THE END
- Your heroine wants to find the buried treasure, and the person who has the map gives it to her. THE END

In other words, without conflict, there is no story. There's nothing for the reader to worry about, there's no reason to root for the characters, there's no emotional fallout one way or the other for the reader.

Conflict: Get some.

52. External conflict vs. internal conflict

One element of story successful writers have mastered is knowing the difference between external and internal conflict, and understanding a good book features both.

External conflict is trouble inflicted on the character from an external source: a hurricane, a boss, or a criminal, for instance. Internal conflict is something the character is in control of, but struggles with: anger issues, the inability to commit or trust, compulsive behavior, or phobias. External conflict can cause internal conflict and vice versa, but there is a difference. For a story to work on multiple levels you need both external and internal conflict, and if they play off each other (anger management issues contribute to problems with a boss, or the inability to trust keeps the character from meeting a lifemate), then your story will be stronger. Ideally, both conflicts should be conquered by the end of the story—in fact, your external conflict should force your character to deal with their internal conflict in some way.

53. How to show internal conflict

Because internal conflict is so important to your story and character, try to show your character's internal conflict in the very first scene:

- If your heroine is afraid of commitment, the first scene might be her driving down the street and seeing her boyfriend looking in the window of a jewelry store.
- If your hero is reluctant to trust, the first scene could be in a bar where buddies are sharing secrets, but he holds back.
- If security means everything to your character, the first scene could show him/her being fired.

Getting the internal conflict on the table right away kills two birds with one stone—the reader knows what's important to your character, and you have an opening scene. (See how all this writing stuff works together?)

54. Point of view

The "point of view" (POV) in a story is basically the person who's telling the story or the person from whose point of view the story is being told, which can change from scene to scene.

In an omnipotent (Godlike) POV, there is a narrator who seems to be in the sky, observing the characters and telling what they're doing, saying, thinking, etc. The omnipotent POV is a bit outdated because it distances the reader from the characters and prevents the reader from truly experiencing the story. Instead the reader is "told" the story by the narrator. The omnipotent POV can work, but it's tricky and why make things harder on yourself?

A more popular POV is first person, in which the narrator of the story is the person the story is about and is happening to: *I* went to the store. A bad thing happened to *me*. One advantage of writing in first-person POV is, frankly, it's fun. It's the most natural way to write, which can seem almost like a stream of consciousness. And books in first-person POV allow a reader to really get into the head of the character. The disadvantages? You have to come up with a character who is so interesting readers will *want* to be in their head for a few hundred pages. And it's hard for the reader to get to know other characters who might be just as crucial to the story. Plus telling a multi-layered story in first person POV will be challenging because your main character won't be privy to everything that's happening.

By far the most common POV used is third person: *Denise* went to the store. A bad thing happened to *her*. At first glance, it might seem third person POV is omnipotent, but you will sprinkle your text with bits of internal monologue to let the reader know they are inside the character's head and experiencing the story from Denise's POV. In omnipotent POV, the narrator is hovering over a room, moving in and out of everyone's head at will and telling things the characters couldn't possibly know were happening to each other. One of the giveaways of omnipotent POV, for example, is a sentence such as 'Denise couldn't have known a murderer lurked just around the corner.'

55. Head-hopping

Try to minimize the number of points of view in a story—only the most important characters should have a POV. I prefer to limit POV to three characters, but it's a matter of author choice. Some popular writers give a POV to lots of characters, including minor "walk-on" characters. That style of writing can work, but the writer risks losing or confusing the reader by giving page to characters who don't matter and take time away from characters who do matter.

If you do use multiple points of view, try to stick to one POV per scene or chapter. If you jump from one person's POV to another person's POV in the same scene, it's known as "head-hopping"—it's distracting to a reader and dilutes your writing because the reader doesn't get the chance to stay in one character's head long enough to get to know the character.

Head-hopping is the sign of a beginning writer and—okay, I'll say it—a lazy veteran writer. It's easier to head-hop than to show what the non-POV characters might be thinking through body language and dialogue.

56. Even more on POV

When it comes to point of view (POV), there are times to break rules for effect. For example, while I advise against changing POV in a scene, doing so in a love scene to show what the other character is thinking/feeling can be powerful. But if you switch POV mid-scene, try to stay in the second character's POV for the duration of the scene, versus hopping back and forth.

Also, some authors "mix" POV, such as writing one character's POV in first person, and other characters' POV in third-person POV (in separate chapters). It's a technique to make the reader feel closer to one character, while letting the reader in on things the main character might not know about. Mixing POV's can be effective, but it's a more challenging way to tell a story. I don't recommend mixing POV's in your first attempt at writing a novel, but do be aware of how manipulating POV affects your storytelling.

TIME OUT!

Whew, we've covered a lot of information and you might be feeling overwhelmed. Don't! All of the disparate pieces will start to make sense after a while; soon you'll be integrating them seamlessly without thinking about it. Give yourself time to soak it all in and fold everything into your memory banks. Then take a deep breath, rehydrate, and get back in the game!

57. Setting

The setting for your book can affect so many parts of your story—your characters' outlook on life (small-town values or big-city ambition), their mood (they love brisk temperatures or they worship the sun), the pacing of your story (laid-back beach time or rapid heartbeat of an urban setting), even your cover (cheery seascape or spooky forest).

The most important thing to keep in mind when you choose a setting for your story is whether the setting supports the story in a creative way. Sometimes the setting is simply for reference and logistics, but why not make it part of the story if you can? Will it ratchet up the conflict if you send a bona fide city girl camping? If you take a forest-survivalist and put him in the inner city? A murder in a small community is a different story than a murder in a densely-populated city.

Once you have your plot and characters defined, choose a setting that will enhance your story and will, in effect, become a character of the story itself.

58. Mother Nature

Similar to setting, the weather could and should affect your storyline. Let's say your story involves tracking a serial killer. Think of how your story changes if it takes place during the dog days of summer versus the blizzard of the century. Or maybe the community in your story torn apart by a racially charged crime has to find a way to come together when a tornado sets down and destroys their school. Or perhaps your uptight heroine has planned every detail of her grand wedding, and a monsoon descends.

Overlay the following situations on your story to see if they amp up the conflict:

- A drought
- A flood
- An earthquake
- A wildfire
- A swarm of insects
- A water-borne disease

59. Time period

The vast majority of novels are set in contemporary times, but many authors choose to write in different time periods, either past or future. The time period can add another element of conflict or ratchet up the stakes of your plot.

Take, for instance, a heroine who would rather be a doctor than marry one. That story set in contemporary times presents one set of conflicts, but set the story in the late 1800s, and suddenly you have an entirely different set of conflicts, and quite a different story.

If you set your novel in the future, you'll have more control over the "world" you construct for your characters because anything is possible. But know you'll have to work harder to make an unfamiliar world believable to the reader.

60. How current events affect your story

In my *Southern Roads* romance series, three brothers reunite to rebuild their hometown in the Georgia Mountains that was wiped away by a tornado ten years ago. I envisioned the brothers enlisting an army of men, then when the men threaten mutiny because there are no women, the brothers advertise for women with a pioneering spirit to move there and help rebuild the town. When I pitched it to my publishing house, the senior editor said, "I don't think anyone would buy the fact that the town was completely wiped away by a tornado."

I had to temper my reaction; of all the story elements in my pitch I thought I might get pushback from, the demolition power of a tornado wasn't one of them. I assured her it was plausible, and reminded her it was a small, remote town. She begrudgingly approved my idea, and I went off to write a trilogy.

The same month the first *Southern Roads* book was released, killer tornadoes decimated towns in the Midwest and the South, literally erasing entire towns. Some readers commented I'd taken advantage of the situation, but of course anyone familiar with traditional book publishing knows the books have to be written and in the pipeline months ahead of publication date. It was truly an unfortunate case of life imitating art.

A friend of mine wrote a story about a princess hiding from the paparazzi; it was already in the schedule and the publisher was excited about it. Then Princess Diana was killed in a car accident fleeing paparazzi. The book was cancelled and my friend not only lost a year of work, but the hole in her release schedule affected the momentum of her career. Several times in the past few years, reports have leaked about TV episodes cancelled because they too closely mirrored something tragic that occurred suddenly in real life.

It's a risk every novelist takes when they release a story—that some portion of it will manifest into reality and it will appear you exploited the act.

OR you could take a different tack and be known as the writer who "rips stories from the headlines." If you do, to protect yourself, change and/or flip enough aspects of the story to make it your own.

61. Incorporating technology into your story

I cringe when I think of someone reading books I wrote early in my career that are still in circulation. In the late 1990s, email was scarce and the World Wide Web was in its infancy. Cell phones were available, but scant enough to still be referred to as "car phones" and "cellular phones." Boom boxes and pagers were all the rage, and laptops were an expensive (and cumbersome) luxury.

My, how times have changed! Smart phones are commonplace and social media has permeated our lives. Household appliances and vehicles are high-tech, too, and online retail stores have made it possible to locate and purchase virtually anything from anyplace in the world.

In some ways, technology makes it easier to tell a story—if a character needs to speak to another character, their voice and face is a button-push away. And if voice-to-voice communication isn't necessary, there's text and email. It's easier for your characters to research things, too, because they have countless databases at their fingertips.

But technology can also cause problems for writers. If, for example, you need for a character to be isolated and vulnerable, it's no longer enough for her to have a flat tire on the side of the road and be obliged to accept help from a dangerous stranger. For the scene to work, her phone would have to be dead and the charger in her car disabled, as well as the car's satellite communications system. And that's assuming she doesn't have a portable charger in her purse.

Technology has also made it harder on crime writers—it's more and more difficult to pull off a perfect crime, from advancements in fingerprinting and DNA, to electronic footprints and alibis created by suspects as their credit cards, GPS systems, and phones are tracked.

Incorporating technology into your contemporary story is a must—you can't escape it. But being too specific about equipment and capability can date your story. A writer has to walk a fine line between general-use devices and cutting-edge technology.

62. A selling title

The title of your novel could be the most important aspect of your book package. Because even if you've written a fantastic story, it needs a memorable, selling title to help people actually find it.

I've sold books based on a title alone: *Our Husband, Party Crashers, In Deep Voodoo, Body Movers*, and others. A title has to achieve a lot in very few words. A good title should accomplish one or more of the following tasks:

- Hints at the storyline—The title should give the reader some idea of what the book is about: *Message in a Bottle, The Tale of Peter Rabbit, The Happy Hooker*.
- Conveys the tone of the book—The title should suggest a mood— spooky, spiritual, comedic, suspenseful: *Gone Girl, Guilty Wives, Twilight*
- Evokes an image—The title should evoke an image in the reader's mind, most easily achieved by including a concrete noun in your title: *The Kite Runner, The Girl Who Kicked the Hornet's Nest, The Orphan Train*
- Is memorable—The title includes unusual words, or an unusual juxtaposition of words: *Water for Elephants, A Feast for Crows, The Fault in Our Stars*
- Is discoverable—The title includes a keyword readers might search for: ***Alien** Hunters, The **Mystery** of the Old Clock, Mrs. Smith's **Romance***

If a great title comes to you before or while you're developing your storyline, that's great—a terrific title can be good motivation for getting a story underway. But don't get married to your book title until you're finished writing the manuscript; be open if other (better) titles emerge during the writing process.

63. Title DON'Ts

Things to avoid when titling your novel:

DON'T choose a title that's been overused. Titles in the United States aren't copyrightable, which is why you see titles repeated within and across the book, music, and movie industry. Perform a search for your proposed title to see how many other properties will be sharing your search results page.

DON'T include words in your title that are difficult to spell or pronounce. Remember, most readers will be buying your book online; it would be a shame to miss out on sales because readers can't recall/spell your title.

DON'T include trendy words. Incorporating fashionably hip words (Hashtag, LOL, Selfie) into your novel's title will quickly date your book.

Your title will be the single most identifiable aspect of your novel—choose it wisely.

64. More about titles

Once you select your title, try to integrate it into your story, either in dialogue or internal monologue, or into the plot itself. When I wrote my romantic comedy titled *My Favorite Mistake* (not original, by the way, but fitting), throughout the story, I emphasized the title by highlighting "mistakes" in the plot: the main character made a big mistake by marrying a guy in a quickie Vegas marriage, which she had annulled. Then they are reunited through a tax audit which she thinks is triggered by mistakes she made on the form. On and on, the theme of making mistakes and finding redemption from those mistakes is layered as the story unfolds.

Here are some examples of titles of my books and how I made them work hard:

Got Your Number—A woman is being stalked by someone who leaves her a menacing message that they've "got her number"—i.e., they know about a secret she's kept. Also, the two women in the book go on a road trip to accomplish numbered items on a life list they created years ago. And there's a guy in the story who literally wants the main character's number (as in phone number).

I Think I Love You—Three sisters estranged because of one man reunite to reveal details about a murder they witnessed when they were young. The idea of being unsure of love is seen in different relationships in the book—between the sisters, their parents (who are divorcing), the one man they all loved at some time in their life, and the possibility of new romantic relationships.

Kill the Competition—Four women carpool from the suburbs of Atlanta to their jobs downtown and are implicated in a murder at their office building. The sense of competition is explored throughout the story on lots of levels—between the women themselves, between the main character and her female boss, between two men who vie for the heroine's attentions. And in the heroine's mind, the life (and man) she left in Ohio are competing against the new life she's trying to build for herself in Atlanta.

Remember to look for ways to make your title an integral part of the story.

65. Writing the back cover blurb

Writing a back cover blurb will help you encapsulate the basic setup of your book—you don't have to say yet how it ends, just the conflict and the hook. Don't know how to write a back cover blurb? Go to your bookshelf and read the back cover blurbs of books you own and ask yourself what about the blurb prompted you to buy the book. Write a blurb for your story in less than 300 words (actual blurbs are much shorter). Your blurb should:

- Describe the high concept of the story
- Give the reader some information about the main character
- Hint, tease, lure, and titillate the reader into buying the book

Make your book blurb exciting and irresistible! The back cover blurb is your promise to the reader your book is worth the cover price. And avoid spoilers—you want your reader to buy the book to find out what happens.

66. Tone

Tone is one of those elements of writing that's difficult to describe. Many writers infuse a tone into their story without conscious effort or knowledge. Your book might have a comedic tone, for example, or a suspenseful tone, or a scary tone. Tone is very similar to voice, except a writer has only one voice, but can write different books that have different tones. Take care to ensure your book maintains the same tone throughout the story. Your reader is taking cues from every aspect of your story as to what they can expect and how they should feel. If you begin writing a story with a light tone and it suddenly veers into a dark, suspenseful tone, your reader will be confused. Changing or skipping around in tone is a mistake beginning writers make, and can occur if you don't know what type of book you're writing, or if you set it aside and come back to it later when you're in a different frame of mind. Tone is an element of story readers typically don't notice unless it's uneven or shifting. You should strive to have the tone of your story sensed but not noticed.

One last note about tone: The tone of your story should match the subject matter. You probably don't want to tackle a dark subject matter with a light tone that might come across to the reader as inappropriate. And if you do, know that you have to do it well.

67. Fashionably downbeat

Many beginning writers feel a sense of responsibility to say something important or deep or meaningful. Indeed, books and movies that receive the most accolades are the ones that stir our conscience or delve into dark elements of the human psyche. The temptation to write a story with a fashionably downbeat tone or ending can be compelling. And if your natural voice or inclination is to write stories about characters who are struggling with unsettling or taboo situations such as depression, abuse, addiction, criminal behavior, etc., then you should follow your instincts. But don't get caught in the trap of believing in order for your story to be important or sellable, it has to be heavy in subject matter or tone.

68. Themes—and do you need one?

Most successful books and movies have a theme, meaning an underlying motif that drives the storyline. Earlier when I talked about integrating your title into your story, I mentioned for my romantic comedy *My Favorite Mistake*, mistakes are a recurring theme. Similarly, your story theme might be about forgiveness, or second chances, or starting over. Other popular themes include honesty, competition, loyalty, redemption, overcoming adversity, and justice.

Your story doesn't have to have a theme, but it probably does and you simply haven't noticed. If you do identify or introduce a theme, look for ways to layer it into the plot in different aspects of the characters' lives.

69. Imagery

Writers are prone to using imagery in stories, but imagery is another one of those elements you might weave into your plot inherently as a storyteller and be unaware of it. Once you realize you're utilizing imagery, you will be closer to mastering it.

Imagery is using one thing (usually something visible or concrete) to indicate another thing (usually something abstract). For example, in the movie *Forest Gump*, a floating feather leads the viewer from one time period to another, a reminder that everything is tied together. Nature is a popular source of imagery: water, weather, the change of seasons, etc., but you can draw imagery from anywhere. In my novel *Kill the Competition*, the infamous Atlanta traffic symbolized and reflected what was going on in the heroine's life.

Movies have an advantage over books where imagery is concerned because they are a visual medium. In a book, a writer has to be more subtle to weave imagery into a story—you don't want your hero saying, "Hm, this drought seems to mirror the fact that my resources have dried up." You're more clever than that.

70. Does your book have a message?

Readers generally enjoy reading because it's a way for them to experience something without having to endure it. In other words, they enjoy living vicariously through your characters. So when a character learns to forgive a parent who was cold or indifferent, the reader will probably come away with a better understanding of a similar relationship in their own life. In that sense, every novel has a message, whether it be uplifting or cautionary: *If you do this, that will happen.*

But you might have a goal to impart a more specific message to your reader: correcting stereotypes or persuading them to support or disavow a cause. Folding a message into your story is fine, but consider using a light hand. I stopped reading one hugely popular writer because his books became too preachy for my tastes on topics he obviously felt very passionate about. If you tackle a divisive topic in your book, consider showing both sides of the issue through characters who are equally ardent about their perspective. Perhaps your main character isn't swayed to the opposing side, but comes to have empathy for those who believe differently.

71. Is writing to formula a good or a bad thing?

Previously I mentioned becoming familiar with the basic tenets and various flavors of your genre. It's crucial to know what elements readers will expect. For example, romance readers expect a happy ending. Mystery readers expect the crime to be solved. Science fiction readers expect your story to impart information about life in the future.

In addition, readers in a particular genre will expect certain plot turns: Romance readers expect to meet a hero and a heroine, then see an evolution of their relationship that will include obstacles and missteps and setbacks before the inevitable resolution of the relationship. Mystery readers expect to be presented with a crime, a list of suspects, an investigator (professional or amateur), red herrings, and an apex of action where the guilty party is revealed. These elements are sometimes referred to as a "formula" and in some circles, "formulaic" is code for "unoriginal." But know that writing to formula is both a safety net and challenging at the same time. On one hand, knowing readers' expectations puts you way ahead of the game; on the other hand, adhering to a formula while delivering a fresh story, characters, setting, and plot twists is a tall order.

72. Building your "world"

The term "world-building" typically indicates the creation of a world that's unfamiliar to the reader, perhaps a society/climate that existed in the past, that could exist in the future, or might exist in an alternate universe. In a world that involves fantasy, magic, horror, or any paranormal elements, you should invest time in establishing the rules of your world. For example, who in your world has power, the "pecking order" of power-holders, what is necessary for a character to wield their power, what threatens their power, and if there's a cost of using their power.

But even if you set your story in the present, you need to create a world for your characters to exist in, and the more unusual the world (the world of Formula One racing, the world of art collecting, the world of competitive eating), the more research and planning you'll have to put into your world to make if feel authentic and accessible to the reader.

73. Write a working synopsis

A synopsis is an overview of the entire book, from the beginning to the end, including all major plot points. Some writers say they don't write a synopsis because it takes all the fun out of writing the book. If you enjoy false starts, writing pages you'll never use, hitting dead ends, backtracking, pulling out your hair, fits of crying, and throwing things, then skip ahead to section 80. If, however, you want to increase your odds of successfully reaching "The End" and having a decent book to show for it, then keep reading.

Good, you're still with me. My working synopsis is the roadmap I follow to keep me focused. Every minute I spend on the synopsis working out timeline and plot kinks will save me days—maybe *weeks*—of time and vexation in the actual writing process. If you plan to submit your book to a publisher, you'll have to write a synopsis anyway, so take the time to do the exercise up front to get the most out of it.

If you still insist knowing the end of the book will take all of the fun out of writing the story then consider this: Your goal as a working writer is to be able to sell a book before you write it—and no editor is going to buy a book without knowing how it ends.

My working synopsis is typically about ten pages long. Plan to spend several days on your synopsis—this is where you play "what-if" games and brainstorm your story. Here is where you'll make notes to yourself of what elements you want to include, and maybe items you need to research. Of course the story and characters might take different turns when you actually write the chapters, but that's okay— your working synopsis is only a guide to keep you on track. Treat your working synopsis like a living entity—it will probably grow and shrink and change as you write your book, but it should remain your compass throughout the process.

74. More about your synopsis

Thinking ahead to writing a selling synopsis to accompany your manuscript to an editor's desk and will be *much* shorter than your working synopsis, keep in mind the editor will want to know three things:

1. who your interesting characters are
2. what interesting situation you're going to put them in
3. how the interesting situation will change your interesting characters

The last one is where most writers (and synopses) fall short. Make sure your working synopsis covers the evolution of your characters so when it comes to writing a shorter selling synopsis later, you won't be scrambling—or rethinking your story.

75. How to make your story more epic

If you'd like to elevate the scope and stakes of your story, simply insert the media! A story can go national and/or global with only a little exposure. You can add a character who's a reporter or a blogger or a social media expert to interact with other characters and act as a conduit to the rest of the world. You can also make your story more epic if you include elements shared by large populations, such as a national holiday, natural disaster, or a global event such as a sporting competition, medical epidemic, or political conference.

76. What Really Happened

If you're working on a thriller or a mystery novel, it's helpful to write a chunky paragraph about WHAT REALLY HAPPENED. Because when you're trying to plant red herrings and keep your reader guessing with twists and turns, it's easy to get to the end of a manuscript and realize you don't quite have it all worked out in your head yet, or you've planted so many obstacles, the end you envisioned is no longer plausible. By keeping WHAT REALLY HAPPENED in front of me, I don't inadvertently clobber or over-complicate my finale, and I don't have to backtrack and rewrite to make it all work.

77. Timeline

Give some serious thought to the time span your book will encompass. Shorter timelines = faster pacing. With that in mind, it's probably best to accelerate your story timeline compared to how long the same situation would unfold in real life. For example, in real life, processing DNA from crime scenes takes weeks, even months. But if you adhere to a realistic timeline in your thriller, you're going to reduce the thrill considerably. Ditto for romances—the typical real-life romance is drawn out as the people go through the stages of dating, engagement, then matrimony. But a contemporary romance novel needs to sparkle with excitement, so falling in lust/love quickly is paramount to the pacing and storytelling.

Double-check the timeline of your story in your synopsis. Make sure women aren't pregnant for ten months, for example. And remember certain things can't happen on certain days. In one of my books, the heroine checked her mailbox every day for an important letter/package, so I had to accommodate days when the mail doesn't run.

78. Create a chapter outline

Once I have my working synopsis, which can be long and unwieldy, I will separate it into a chapter outline. I plan for 10-15 pages per chapter, so for a 350-page manuscript, that's about 30 chapters. I begin breaking up the working synopsis into those 30 chapters. Next to the chapter number, I put in how much time elapses in the chapter (Friday morning to Saturday evening, for example), and if I have more than one point of view in the book, I list which character(s) point of view will be used. When I'm finished, a chapter heading might have a paragraph underneath, another chapter heading might have a single sentence, and some chapter headings will be blank. That's okay because I'll fill in the blanks as I keeping working and expanding the synopsis/outline.

79. Color-coding your outline

In the chapter outline, I sometimes use color-coded fonts to track elements of the story. For example, in my *Body Movers* mystery series, there are three potential love interests for the main character, Carlotta. I work hard to try to give each man a fair share of page. One way to ensure I haven't neglected one of the men in the story is to assign a different color to each man, and any time one of the men is in a scene, I use that color to highlight it in the chapter outline. That way, at a glance I can tell if I need to give the men more or fewer scenes. You can use the same technique to track themes, imagery, red herrings, or the evolution of a relationship.

80. Imagination drill!

A woman bursts into a boardroom, walks up to the man giving a presentation, and slaps his face. Why? Can you come up with 10 scenarios?

1.

2.

3.

4.

5.

6.

7.

8.

9.

10.

(For printable PDFs of all Imagination Drills, go to
www.stephaniebond.com.)

81. Plotster vs. pantster

There are generally two categories of writers: plotsters and pantsters. Plotsters plan, plan, plan. Conversely, pantsters (i.e., write by the seat of their pants) start with a basic story concept, then sort of figure things out as they go along.

I confess I'm a hardcore plotster—I derive satisfaction from writing efficiently and I believe being a plotster has allowed me to write a lot of novels and deliver them on-schedule. One drawback of being a plotster, though, is you run the risk of following your plan too rigidly, and ignoring the little surprises that pop up along the way that could enrich your story. Revisions for plotsters will probably revolve around layering in characterization and adding atmospheric details.

What pantsters sacrifice in efficiency, they gain in spontaneity. Pantsters thrive on the thrill of the unknown, and their stories can feel wonderfully fresh, but they risk 1) not delivering the book the editor is expecting and 2) not delivering on time. Revisions for pantsters will probably revolve around plugging plot holes.

I have seen writers change tack under duress—I can remember a couple of times I went the pantster route when writing a short project under a very tight timeframe and the plot was so straightforward there was almost nowhere it could go wrong. Conversely, I've seen pantsters get a few books into their career and decide they want to move toward the plotster end of things to streamline the writing process a bit.

82. "I can't believe that just happened!"

When you're plotting your book, I suggest you drop in at least one scene or plot twist that will leave the reading saying, "I can't believe that just happened!" It can't come completely out of the blue, of course—it has to be organic to the story and the characters. And perhaps it's hinted at in a previous chapter, but imbedded so deeply into narrative the reader didn't think it was important. When "it" happens, it should surprise—even shock—but it should make sense.

83. Should you write a series?

Let me say up front that readers love, love, *love* series, so if you feel inclined to write a series, you should follow your instincts. If you intend to self-publish your books, you can release books as often as you can produce them, with no impediments. But if you intend to pursue publication at a traditional publishing house, you should know that while publishers acknowledge the appeal of series, the fate of your series will be in their hands. (Take it from someone who's had three series cut short by publishers, leaving readers frustrated and angry.)

To create a series, you'll need an over-arching element to tie all the books together. A mystery series generally features the same crime-solver(s). A romance series might feature the members of one family, or be set in one community. A science fiction series typically features a more epic continuing storyline, such as a war of worlds. Series can also revolve around popular hobbies such as cooking, collecting, travel, or around interesting vocations such as dog-walker, wedding planner, or hotel concierge. You can build a series around anything you want, as long as it's compelling and offers enough flexibility to encompass a few/several/many stories. If you're a history buff, you might consider setting a series in a time gone by, which opens up an entirely new set of possibilities.

84. Create a series bible

If you do decide to write a series, or even two connected books, it's a good idea to establish a series bible. The series bible is simply a reference guide to keep track of:

- series title and explanation of elements that tie the books together
- individual book titles and story blurbs
- character names, descriptions, and pertinent details such as quirks, hobbies, or speech patterns
- setting, including landmarks, weather, and atmospheric details
- buildings and descriptions/layouts
- timelines
- outstanding issues to resolve

Maintaining a comprehensive series bible will be invaluable as you progress through books in the series and details you swore you'd never forget become fuzzy.

85. Including holidays in your story

Another element you might consider adding to your story is a holiday that re-volves around family or relationships: New Year's, Valentine's Day, Mother's Day, Father's Day, Fourth of July, Halloween, Thanksgiving, Christmas, Hanukkah. Holidays heighten emotion and can move the needle in either direction where familial or romantic relationships are concerned. Holidays can also bring with them a sense of obligation to uphold certain traditions and rituals that create their own conflict. And did I mention readers love holiday stories?

86. Research

Each time a reader opens a book, they are agreeing to an implied contract with the author to *suspend their inclination to disbelieve* for the duration of the story. In other words, they are agreeing to believe what you've written, to go along for the ride. In order to encourage your reader's "suspension of disbelief," you'll have to demonstrate some knowledge of your subject matter. To that end, there will be details you'll have to research—the setting, a character's occupation, and countless other facts. If an important aspect of the story is jarringly incorrect, your reader will begin to critique the story rather than enjoy it.

With the Internet, there are infinite sources for research—articles, images, videos. But keep in mind other writers are using the same sources, so you might have to dig a little deeper in the search results to find that unique nugget of information to set your story apart.

87. Writing about what you don't know

There's an old writing adage to "write what you know." But there will be times when you'll have to write about what you don't know, and looking up something online isn't going to tell you enough to be able to fake it. But you're in luck because industry experts are now more accessible than ever through blogs, podcasts, videos, and books. Most industries have their own trade publications which you might be able to subscribe to, or buy on the secondary market through online sites. And most organizations, including law enforcement agencies, have public relations departments to field questions. Also, ask about public education programs, such as open house events or citizen ride-alongs. If you want to find out more about court proceedings, most local hearings are open to the public. If you need an "inside person" for information, you might consider going online to find a resource on social media, or go on social media and ask if anyone can help. Just remember to be gracious to your source and/or be prepared to pay for their services if they charge by the hour. A thank you note or edible gift is also a nice gesture. And don't forget to send them a signed copy of your finished novel!

88. Story incubation

I do some of my best thinking in the shower. Incubating a story is an essential step to developing characters and plotlines before committing them to paper. The story incubation phase is the time to let your mind wander, to take idea fragments down paths and over walls and through the middle of a busy street. Go on—you don't have to use any of it in your story…but something amazing just might float into your mind. Freeform thinking allows your subconscious to take over and present to you tidbits you've tucked away, or connect unrelated details in a magical way. Water is my imagination trigger—swimming, floating, soaking…even cleaning turns up the incubation temperature and allows my ideas to flourish. Find *your* trigger.

89. Collage your story

One technique I use to help gel characters, setting, and other aspects of a story in my mind is to build a collage. A collage can be physical, such as a manila folder or poster board, or electronic, such as a Pinterest board, but the idea is to take pictures and images, words, etc., to build a visual world for my book, including pictures of the main characters, buildings, scenery, and objects important to the story. I refer to the collage while I'm writing the book to jog my memory. This is an especially helpful exercise when I'm working on more than one project at once. When I'm ready to write (or to resume writing), opening the collage is like opening a window onto my story. Collaging is a fun project to do with friends, family, readers, and other writers.

90. Design a mockup of your book cover

Another visual motivator to get your story underway is to design a mockup of your book cover. Coming up with an image, background, and title for your book requires you to really think about your story...and requires you to start thinking about what you want to convey to your reader. Is there an object in your story—a piece of jewelry, a building, a tree, a map—that plays a prominent part in the plot? (If not, this might be a good time to build in a visual element that would lend itself to a cover.) Keep in mind this isn't an exercise to create the actual cover for your book, so it doesn't have to be perfect—this is only a pre-writing exercise to help you get your story in focus.

91. Setting up files to manage your novel

Over the years I've developed a filing system/group of files to help me manage a book. Every book gets its own folder, then within each folder, I have the following document files:

- BLURB—the back cover blurb
- SYNOPSIS—the working synopsis
- CHAPTER OUTLINE—the working synopsis, broken down by chapter
- PEOPLE AND PLACES—list of characters, buildings, scene venues
- CHAPTER TEMPLATE—a skeleton template, already formatted
- COVER MOCKUP and COLLAGE (if created electronically)
- DON'T FORGET—details I think of along the way I don't want to inadvertently leave out, or things I mentioned early in the book, but need to tie up
- EXTRAS—unused scenes to save and possibly recycle

Additionally, I'll create a spreadsheet file PAGECOUNT, where I keep up with how many pages I've written, and how many pages are in each chapter, so I can tell at a glance which chapters are lean and which chapters might be flabby.

READY...SET...GO!

You've dreamed about this day, and you've put in your training time...now let's see what you've got!

92. The first step is the heaviest

If you've always wanted to write a novel but to this point haven't yet started, let today be the day you type "Chapter 1," and begin telling your story. Remember, every novelist in history had doubts and hesitations and detractors and distractions. But they forged ahead, starting with one word that grew into one sentence that grew into one paragraph that grew into one page that grew into one chapter that grew into one book...and some of those books became literary icons. The first step is usually the hardest to take, but afterward you might discover the goal/task isn't as overwhelming as you built it up to be in your mind. Remember, that's what writers do in our minds—we puff things up...embellish...exaggerate. Don't let that overactive imagination of yours prevent you from setting your dream of being a novelist into motion.

93. How to begin a story

If you're struggling with how to start your novel, consider dropping the reader into the middle of a conversation—dialogue is always more interesting to read than narrative. Starting with someone asking a question can be particularly intriguing. On the other hand, an example of what might not be the best way to begin a commercial fiction novel is with the main character alone, thinking, or worse—*remembering*. It's important that you grab the reader right away and draw them into the story, and it's hard to do that when the character is being passive. Lots of readers skim the first page of a novel before deciding whether to buy it—you have only a few paragraphs to prove your story is going somewhere. (By the way, editors often make their buying decisions the same way!)

94. The first line of your novel

Take some time to consider the first line of your story. Ideally, the first line should resonate with the tone of your story: humorous, serious, poignant, etc. As I mentioned earlier, dropping the reader into the middle of a conversation is a great way to open a novel:

"I'll need your answer by five o'clock today."
"My best guess is you have six months to live."
"The truth is, I want a divorce."

Your opening doesn't have to start with dialogue, but it should be punchy. Here are some great opening lines from books I chose from my bookshelf:

In the car lot of life, Amanda Sheridan decided, she was a Volvo station wagon with about eighty thousand miles on it. *—Single in Suburbia*, Wendy Wax

The woman had no face. *—Don't Say a Word*, Rita Herron

Marissa Vasquez had known her escape from prison was too good to be true. *—Bride of the Wolf*, Jennifer St. Giles

The first line of your novel should pique the imagination of the reader, make them ask, "Where is this story going? I want to keep reading to find out."

95. Backstory

Note that most writers begin writing *before* the story actually begins. Don't frontload your novel with backstory—start your novel just before something changes in your main character's life. Not a year before, not six months before, not a week before, but more like *minutes* before something happens to set them off on their adventure. And all those great details you've built into the character's backstory? Feed those to the reader a little at a time as the story progresses. We don't need to be in love with your character from the get-go—he/she can grow on us.

96. Page one—manuscript format

There is no one exact format for a manuscript, but the basic format is 1 - 1 1/4" margins all around, double-spaced, and a 12-point font (most used are Courier and Times New Roman). Play around with your word processor to add a page header to your document that contains your title, your name, and the page number. If you have a header, you won't need a footer. If you're starting a new chapter, tab to about halfway down the page to center the words "Chapter 1," then tab another couple of times, indent your first (and subsequent) paragraphs, and start writing!

For each book I create a skeleton document as CHAPTER TEMPLATE, then pull up/import the template file to begin a new chapter.

97. Do you need a prologue?

You probably don't need a prologue. Here's why: You need to get into the story as quickly as possible, and when you write a prologue, you delay entry. Prologues are a writerly device that novelists, especially new novelists, like to employ. But readers don't love them; in fact, just seeing the word "prologue" seems to be a turn off. Some readers don't even read the prologue; they treat it like a "foreword" or a note from the author, thinking it's not relevant to the story they are eager *to get into as quickly as possible.*

Editors have the same aversion to prologues. With that in mind, you need a strong reason to write one. Some good reasons for a prologue are: To include a scene that took place before the story begins which has a strong bearing on the story itself. Or to include a scene that takes place in the future and ends on a cliffhanger, then the book begins telling the story that leads up to the scene in the prologue.

Some book elements fall in and out of vogue: prologues, flashbacks, chapter titles, epilogues all have their place, but most have had their day.

98. The setup chapters

The story setup is usually the first 3-5 chapters and ends on a cliffhanger. In the business, this is also known as "sample chapters," or the "proposal." The setup chapters are what an editor will read to decide if they want to read more, so it should be really, really, really good. In the setup, we meet your main character and see their current world, then we see how something threatens their world, and we see the choice they're faced with to respond to the threat. Sounds simple...and it is! Enjoy this phase because writing the setup is kind of the fun part. Indeed, this is where you demonstrate to the reader the story's potential—you should leave the reader's imagination firing in all directions, leave them saying, "I can't wait to see what happens next!"

99. Pesky chapter 4

For me, the hardest part of a story to write is after the setup chapters. After the setup, there's sometimes a feeling of "Okay, what now?" The "what now?" part might seem overwhelming because it's time for the character to begin their long journey back to where they were before the incident that changed their life, or perhaps journey to a better place. It's okay to feel overwhelmed at this point—try to channel that frustration to your character who should also be wondering "What now?" Then do what everyone has to do when faced with an overwhelming task: push through it.

Have I mentioned the failure rate for writers is astronomically high? I have lots of writer friends who have many manuscripts they've begun, but abandoned after the first few chapters because they didn't work through "what now?" It's easy to put a character in hot water, it's much more difficult to get them out. By pushing through this tough spot in your story, you will already set yourself apart from most aspiring writers.

100. Pacing

You can control the pacing of your story with the length of your chapters: Longer chapters draw out the story, shorter chapters are best for action-packed scenes. I try to keep my chapters to about 10-12 manuscript pages, and shorter if the story calls for it. Readers like short-ish chapters because it gives them a readable chunk before bedtime, on their lunch hour, etc. Plus shorter chapters makes your book feel (literally) like a "page-turner." Personally, I like to start a book with shorter chapters, then gravitate toward slightly longer chapters in the "meat" of the story, then speed things up again with shorter chapters toward the end.

101. Whitespace

Another technique for controlling the pace of your story is to monitor the whitespace of your manuscript. An editor once told me she could tell if a submission was worth reading by simply flipping through the pages to see how much whitespace the writer had utilized. Because whitespace indicates two things: dialogue or a change in thought/direction. You've done it yourself as a reader—you become bored with a dense passage in a book, so you skim forward to the next section of whitespace. A long paragraph with extended sentences is slow....meandering...thoughtful. (Useful in an emotional scene.) A short paragraph with pithy sentences is rapid and quick-fire. (Useful in a heated exchange or action scene.)

Control the whitespace in your manuscript by keeping your paragraphs and blocks of dialogue short. Contrary to what your grammar teacher wrote on the blackboard, you don't need a "topic" sentence in every paragraph in fiction. I don't have a set number of sentences or lines I adhere to in a paragraph, but when it creeps past 10 lines or so on my manuscript page, I start looking for a way to either shorten it or break it up.

Whitespace is your friend—it makes your book more approachable to a reader, which sets the tone for enjoying your story.

102. A hard-working chapter

A chapter has to achieve a lot in a short number of pages. A hard-working chapter should:

- **Orient the reader.** It might have been a while since the reader left off reading.
- **Progress the story.** Some part of the story has to be moved forward.
- **Ratchet up the conflict.** Up until the last few chapters, when things should be wrapping up.
- **Leave off on a hook.** So the reader is tempted to turn the page and keep reading.
- **Be a cohesive unit.** Yet function as part of a bigger story.

103. Chapter hooks

I once read a manuscript where every chapter read like a short story, and the chapters were only loosely related. I quickly lost a sense of chronology because, although the chapters were mildly interesting, they weren't moving the story forward, and I had no sense of what the next plot point might be. Each chapter dealt with a different character and usually ended with the character going to sleep. (Which made me want to do the same.)

Your objective is to end the chapter on a "hook" to entice the reader to turn the page. You should also end with something transitional, so the reader knows what will (or might) happen next.

104. Time passage

You don't have to account for every minute in your novel. Showing time passage is my weakness—it's not uncommon for me to be several chapters into a manuscript and realize only a day and a half have passed! The reader needs to get a sense that time is passing and to be oriented as to the day and time. Don't be afraid to write things like "The next morning...." or "She spent the afternoon analyzing records...." in order to move things along. Also, mention the time of day in your scene descriptions—is the sun high? Is it dusk? Is the moon shining?

105. Grammar

If you aspire to be published by a traditional publisher, you might think you don't have to brush up on grammar because, after all, it's the editor's job to edit, right?

Wrong. It's true an editor will still buy your story even if it's not letter-perfect—*if* she loves the story. But sloppy punctuation and bad grammar are jarring and will detract from your story, so why risk it? Brush up on basic grammar with a textbook, stylebook, or a refresher course online. The writing industry is extremely competitive. An editor is probably skimming a dozen or more manuscripts in one sitting. Let's say she reads yours and is intrigued by the story, but notes it's riddled with grammatical problems. And the next manuscript she reads is equally intriguing, but free of grammatical errors…which one do you think she's more likely to buy? Some publishing houses receive 100 submissions per day—your manuscript has to be as polished as you can make it in order to stand out from the slush pile.

106. Grammar vs. expression

So you've been charged with brushing up on good grammar and using it diligently, like a sharpened tool. That said, when you have to choose between getting your point across or breaking a grammar rule, break the grammar rule. For example, I'm fond of using fragmented sentences and made-up words in order to enhance the rhythm of my storytelling, and setting off a single sentence or even a single word in a paragraph by itself for emphasis. Know the rules, and know when to break them. Your priority as a storyteller is first to tell a good story and second, to tell a good story *well*.

107. Imagination drill!

A woman opens her purse, then gasps. Why? Can you come up with 10 scary, creepy, delightful, or shocking things that might be inside?

1.

2.

3.

4.

5.

6.

7.

8.

9.

10.

(For printable PDFs of all Imagination Drills, go to
www.stephaniebond.com.)

108. Dialogue

I'm not above eavesdropping on conversations when I'm out and about just to listen to how people communicate. Eavesdropping on at least one side of a conversation is easy because so many people walk about with a cell phone glued to their ear, shouting at the person on the other end. Here are a few observations I've made about dialogue I apply in my books:

- People generally are poor communicators. They use too many words, use the wrong words, repeat themselves, and talk over each other.
- Teenagers have their own vocabulary, and rarely make eye contact when they talk.
- Men use about 1/10th the number of words women use.
- Men often don't respond to a question or respond with another question.
- Women feel obligated to answer THE question asked, no matter how intrusive or how incriminating their answer might be.
- Women "emote" more than men, saying "I feel" or "in my opinion"; men state things without a caveat.
- Men tend to say more with body language than with words.
- People lie. A lot.

Keeping all of the above in mind, you will have to "pretty up" dialogue to speed things along.

109. More on dialogue

Study dialogue in novels to get a feel for good (and bad) dialogue, and the formatting. Some general rules to keep in mind:

- Use quotation marks at the beginning and end of spoken words.
- Each speaker gets their own paragraph to establish a back and forth rhythm.
- Try to make the dialogue stand alone without dialogue tags.
- If you use dialogue tags, keep them simple—he said and she said are fine.
- Avoid overuse of dialogue tags with adverbs: she said pleadingly, he cried loudly.
- Keep your dialogue brief—no speeches!

The point of view character gets the advantage of thinking and reacting internally to dialogue; for other characters, their dialogue and body language are the only clues to the point of view character (and the reader) as to what they're thinking. Writing good dialogue is harder than you might think, but if your dialogue sparkles, your characters will come alive.

110. Dialect

I grew up in the South, where speech and conversation is a bit more casual than in other parts of the U.S. Luckily, my written English is better than my spoken English, but occasionally I do have characters I want to give a country or Southern dialect. The trouble is, reading dialect where the character talks like this: "How are yew doin' today, sweetie-peach pie?" can be very tedious to a reader. So it's best to strive for giving the reader a *flavor* of the character's speech: "How are you doin' today, sweetie?" Dialect slows down the reader, so use sparingly.

111. Sensuality level

If you're writing a novel that involves romantic relationships, give some thought to the sensuality level of your book. The erotica genre is identified by the explicit sensuality of the content. Conversely, the inspirational genre is earmarked by the absence of sensuality. In almost every other genre and sub-genre, the sensuality level runs the gamut. Here is where your research and comfort level should intersect. If a publisher has suggestions or constraints regarding sexual content, their writing guidelines will say so. But no matter what a publisher is looking for and what's popular or unpopular among readers, you should always write the level of sensuality you are comfortable with. And include sex or love scenes in your story only if they are organic to the plot—anything else will seem gratuitous to the reader.

112. Sensory detail

Sensory detail refers to a detail that stirs one of our five senses:

- **Sight:** Is the setting panoramic? Bleak?
- **Smell:** Is there a pig farm close by? A bakery?
- **Touch:** Does the winter wind cut through a person's skin? Is a lover's hand callused?
- **Taste:** Does your character crave strawberries? Anchovies?
- **Sound:** Does a train run through the town twice a day? Is a neighbor learning to play the saxophone?

Using sensory detail is the most effective way to draw a reader into a scene and make them feel as if they're experiencing the moment rather than reading about it. A sensory element can also double as a recurring theme in your story.

113. Everyday details

When writing your novel, there's a balance to strike when showing everyday, mundane details. You don't have to show your character brushing their teeth and eating breakfast, for instance, unless it's important to the story. That said, don't forget your character is human and prone to all kinds of little mishaps. Examine your plot to see if day-to-day occurrences can move the story forward while making your characters more relatable. The fender bender in the movie *Crossing Lanes* was an inciting incident that spiraled out of control. The heroine's head cold in the movie *You've Got Mail* demonstrated how vulnerable she was after her business closed and gave the hero an excuse to call on her. And the hero's toothache in the movie *Cast Away* exacerbated his dire situation.

114. Polite fiction conversation

Is it just me, or is every other commercial on television about going to the bathroom? Going, going too much, not going enough. Those ads sell a lot of product, but when it comes to writing, there are parts of a character's grooming and everyday activities a writer can skip and the reader will assume things happen, um, *naturally* off-page.

There are exceptions. The few times I've shown a character "relieving" himself or herself, it was important to the plot. For example, in my first romantic comedy, *Irresistible?*, the main character, an artist, visits a law firm that purchased a painting of hers, and when she doesn't see it hanging in public places, she becomes convinced it's hanging in the men's bathroom. She goes in for a peek and when a man comes in, she dunks into a stall and stands on the toilet to escape detection. Chaos ensues. At different times in my *Body Movers* series, the main character, Carlotta Wren, has followed people into bathrooms in hopes of overhearing a conversation or catching them unawares.

So if it works for your plot, use a bathroom scene. Otherwise, give your character some privacy.

115. Curse words

Like the sensuality level, if a publisher has restrictions on language, their writing guidelines will say so. I don't give much thought to swear words—if it occurs to me one would be appropriate in the dialogue I'm writing, I write it. Or I might simply have a character *think* the dirty word. Keep in mind the more often curse words are used, the less their impact. On the other hand, it could be effective if it's part of a character's personality to use a swear word as punctuation—just be aware a little goes a long way.

Don't forget that sometimes "heck" or "darn" can be as effective as a harsher word if it represents an understatement. And it might be more imaginative to invent a replacement for a swear word unique to a character. For instance, in my book *Kill the Competition*, one of the women, who was a dyed-in-the-wool southerner, was fond of saying "good gravy."

TIME OUT!

Are you still with me? Good! Is your adrenaline pumping? Is your story fermenting in the back of your mind? Are you beginning to see the immense possibilities that await you as a novelist? You can do this!

116. Body language

I was reading a book the other day and had a nagging feeling I wasn't *in* the scene with the characters as they conversed. And then it hit me: the author hadn't used body language to hint as to what the characters were thinking and doing as they conversed. For instance, if someone is talking, but is reading the newspaper at the same time, then they're not really interested in the conversation. But if at some point the person puts down the newspaper and gives their attention to the other person, we know something has changed.

Consider the following line of dialogue: "I'm leaving." Now, how does the connotation (and setting) of those two simple words change as the character's body language changes:

- Her arms are full of text books and she's running out the door.
- She's wearing bloody scrubs and fighting a yawn.
- She's packing a suitcase open on the bed.

And facial expressions can tell the reader so much about a character's inner thoughts—a smile, a smirk, a sneer, the widening of one's eyes, the flare of one's nostrils, the bobbing of an Adam's apple, a neck scratch, pulling a hand down one's face, or pinching the bridge of their nose can either reinforce or betray their true feelings.

117. More on body language

If you're like most writers, your novel will probably have a "body movement *du jour*," meaning you will inadvertently use a phrase to describe a character's expression or movement and it will work so well, you'll use it again... and again...and again. If a character has a tic or habitual movement (such as chewing gum or pushing up glasses) that defines him/her, that's okay. Otherwise, try to vary the body language descriptions as much as possible. I keep a long list of common body movements—cracking knuckles, steepling hands, splaying hands, etc.—to refer to when my brain gets fuzzy.

118. Writing love scenes

Your attitude about writing love and/or sex scenes definitely plays a part in how the scenes turn out. If you're tentative about writing them, they'll probably read that way. Here's a checklist to help edit your love scenes:

- Are the transitions (before, during, and after) the scene smooth?
- Are the logistics clear—and believable?
- Is the language appropriate?
- Is the scene told in the point of view of the person who has the most at stake?
- Are the characters behaving "in character"?
- Does the love scene progress the external conflict and/or the internal conflict?
- Is this love scene somehow more important than a prior love scene(s)?
- Is the emotional intensity appropriate for where the characters are in their relationship?
- Does the scene work with the pacing of the story?

119. Catalyst sentences

A catalyst sentence is a sentence that precedes action or sets something in motion. Basically, in one sentence, everything changes for the character/story. Examples of "catalyst" sentences:

- Suddenly, the door burst open.
- The phone rang and the words "City Morgue" came up on the screen.
- In studying her credit card statement, one of the charges stopped her cold.
- Her dog trotted inside, and what Rusty held in his mouth made her breath catch.

Get the idea? If your plot is just lying there, see if a catalyst sentence can bring it to its feet.

120. Definitive sentences

When you think about it, most memorable movies or books have one or two lines that stand out in the viewer's or the reader's memory:

- "Houston, we have a problem." (*Apollo 13*)
- "We're going to need a bigger boat." (*Jaws*)
- My mama always said life is like a box of chocolates—you never know what you're gonna get." (*Forrest Gump*)

Definitive sentences are satisfying to readers because they encapsulate a scene, a feeling, or a revelation into a digestible sound bite—they cue the reader to the relevancy of the scene, and they give the reader something concrete to take away and to share with other readers. Characteristics of definitive sentences:

- A definitive sentence can reflect a turning point for a character.
- A definitive sentence is typically expressed with memorable words or in a memorable way.
- A definitive sentence is usually set apart—at the beginning or end of a paragraph or chapter—for more emphasis.
- A definitive sentence might be repeated throughout the story, and perhaps demonstrate the character's growth.

Think of some of your favorite lines from books and movies and how the absence of those definitive sentences would have changed their impact.

121. Word choice

Keep in mind that writing a novel is really about making hundreds of thousands of word choices. When you choose to use the word "vehicle" instead of "car," you're sending a subliminal message to the reader about the tone and seriousness of your story, about that scene, and/or about your character's vocabulary. One of the great things about writing fiction in English is since our language has influences from so many other cultures and languages, we typically can choose from an array of words to describe one object or situation, each of them with a slightly different connotation. But with choice comes obligation—as a writer, you should strive to express the exact sentiment with the word that fits that particular moment for that particular character for that particular book. Knowing how important word choice can be, you should try to expand your own vocabulary by reading widely and paying attention to new words being folding into our lexicon, especially as new technologies emerge. Note that word choice is especially important in dialogue because it's an indicator of the character's sex, age, education, attitude, and so many other things.

Don't get hung up on word choice to the point that you're obsessing over every sentence, but be aware of how word choice affects your delivery.

122. Boomerang words

There are certain words in the English language that are unusual because they refer to an obscure object, or because of their spelling, or perhaps the usage has gone out of vogue. Since "boomerang" is one such word, I refer to them as boomerang words—words so unique, they jump out at us. The first time we see them, they have impact; but each time after that, the impact is lessened. Boomerang words are measured against the context in which they're being used—if, for example, you're writing a historical novel, you might include lots of what contemporary readers would consider to be boomerang words. Just know unless your book centers around a boomerang word, i.e., *The American Nabob*, use such words sparingly for best effect.

123. Exclamation points

For writers, nothing is as fun to type as the exclamation point! We love it! It shows excitement! Action! Anger! Surprise! Happiness! Drama!

The overuse of exclamation points is also the sign of a beginner writer. It's considered intrusive because when you use an exclamation point, you're shouting how the character feels or shouting to the reader how they're supposed to feel. Your dialogue and exposition should stand on their own, without being propped up with an exclamation point! In prior sections I mentioned how overusing boomerang words and curse words dilute their impact, and the same is true for exclamation points—they should be used judiciously. Some writers limit themselves to one exclamation point per manuscript. Some writers won't use them, period. If you do use an exclamation point, make sure it's for special emphasis, such as a turning point in the story.

124. Using brand names

If you're writing a contemporary novel, you'll probably have to decide at some point whether to use a brand name—or you might unknowingly use a brand name as a generic term. What's wrong with the following sentence?

She shed her levi's, grabbed a kleenex, and headed to the jacuzzi.

At least three things: Levi's®, Kleenex®, and Jacuzzi® are all registered trademarks protected by law. The proper way to write the sentence is to use the generic terms:

She shed her jeans, grabbed a tissue, and headed to the steam bath.

Writers are expected to know which terms are generic and which are trademark protected. Is a company going to come after you if you use their trademark incorrectly? Probably not, although some companies are famous for protecting their brands, no matter how small the infraction. Do your research, and to be safe, when you use trademarks, be neutral or complimentary. If your heroine is strangled with her Levi's and left in the Jacuzzi with the message "You deserved it" scribbled on a Kleenex, you might be getting a call.

125. Including lyrics and song titles

You can use song titles in your book—remember, titles aren't copyrightable in the U.S. But lyrics *are* copyrighted, so don't include them in your book, unless it's a very old song that's fallen into the public domain. In my book *Kill the Competition*, the heroine has moved to Atlanta, Georgia and is wondering if she's made a big mistake. John Mayer wrote a song titled "Why Georgia" that expresses some of those same thoughts. Here's how I dropped in a mention of the song:

"Inside or outside?" Carole asked Belinda as they approached Gypsy Joe's. The place was packed with merry patrons, and John Mayer's "Why Georgia" played over the speakers.

Also, I could've referred to the meaning of the song's lyrics without including them:

Belinda gripped the steering wheel harder as cars streamed around her stalled vehicle, honking and yelling obscenities. Had she made a big mistake by moving here? The lyrics of John Mayer's "Why Georgia" flitted through her mind.

Novelists should be hyper-aware of infringing on someone else's copyright. Do your research, and when in doubt, omit.

126. Style manual

If you're unsure how to format certain words and elements such as titles, texted conversations, etc., consult a copy of a style guide. There are several expert guides used and preferred by journalists and other professional writers. The *Chicago Manual of Style* (CMS) is considered to be the standard for fiction writing. There's an online version of CMS, too, and a forum for posting questions.

127. When to take literary license

Taking literary license, also known as "artistic license," means you're bending the truth in order to tell a better story. When you write fiction, you're sort of taking literary license with everything anyway, or at least you should be, because real life doesn't always make for good fiction. To achieve good fiction, you sometimes have to omit details or invent new ones in order to keep from bogging down the story with unnecessary or distracting facts.

Let's say you're writing about something like moving bodies from crime scenes, which is what I write about in my *Body Movers* mystery series. I've never moved a body from a crime scene, but I've cobbled together information from people who have, things I've read online, and things I've seen on TV/in movies to make it believable to a layperson. A person who actually hauls bodies for a living might take exception to the specific details, but I leave myself wiggle room because my character is new to body moving, so of course she's going to make mistakes. And since I'm writing comedy, I give myself even more leeway.

So if you interview an expert resource and they say, "Oh, a professional would never do that." Well, given the right circumstances, a person can be persuaded or convinced or blackmailed into doing anything. If you need for your character to do something a professional in their position would never do, simply have you character acknowledge what they're about to do is totally over-the-top. Your task as a novelist is to take a situation and make it seem real enough to be believable, but not so real that the reader feels as if they're reading a documentary.

128. Know your character's world

Previously I mentioned knowing the world in which your story is set, but here I'd like to reinforce how important it is to know your *character's* world, especially if they are of a different age than you are and more especially if you are writing for a different age group than your own. It's certainly important to know how your character would talk and the vocabulary they would use, but it's also important to know what kind of clothes they wear, their preferred method of communication, what kind of entertainment they seek out, what kind of transportation they use, the food they eat, and their general attitude toward health and exercise, sex and nudity. Reality shows are a great way to observe people of varying age groups in an unscripted environment.

129. Relevant cultural references

When you write your story, you should mention enough cultural references to make your story seem real. If your story is set in another time period, you have more leeway, but even if you set your story in the past, you should look up what was going on in the world at that time in case you can fold some of the details into your plot.

If your story is set in contemporary times, you have to find a balance between mentioning enough technology and pop culture references to lend authenticity to your book, but not so much that it feels dated. For example, you might reference the popularity of reality television without mentioning specific shows. Or you might refer to social media platforms generically instead of naming one individually.

(Exception: If you're planning to self-publish, you will have the opportunity to update your story at any time.)

130. Use specific nouns

Avoid using vague nouns such as: *this, that, these, those*, and *it*. Be specific. When you use vague nouns, you set up a weak foundation for your writing because without specific nouns, you can't use specific adjectives. Take this paragraph, for example:

My father owned a red convertible. That is how my family went to town on weekends when I was a girl. This is still a fond memory of mine because I met the man I would marry at the soda shop. He always made triple-decker banana splits, one each for me and my baby sister, garnished with an extra cherry. Those were the highlight of our trip.

In reading the previous paragraph, an editor might stop and frown, or perhaps circle and write "condense" or simply make a mental note that she's not being pulled into the story. Why? Because the nouns are vague and, therefore, not vivid enough to engross the reader. And without vivid nouns, you have no way to insert vivid adjectives. Vague nouns lead to choppy, unsatisfying sentences. See how much cleaner and more intriguing the paragraph reads with specific nouns:

My father owned a red convertible, which provided my family's transport into town on the weekends. Those jaunts are still a fond memory of mine because I met the man I would marry at the soda shop. He always made triple-decker banana splits, one each for me and my baby sister, garnished with an extra cherry. Those piled-high treats were the highlight of our trip.

See the difference? A reader will, too.

131. Show and tell

"Show, don't tell" is one of the oldest pieces of advice in the writing industry, and usually it's true. For example, if during the entire story the hero acts like a jerk toward the heroine, then at the end, declares his love for her, everyone (including the heroine, hopefully), would be pretty skeptical. You/he has to show somewhere along the way his feelings are moving away from jerkdom toward true affection by his actions, by *showing* his feelings, even if he doesn't express them. Likewise, telling the reader the character enjoyed a party is okay, but showing her at the party dancing barefoot is much more powerful. That is, of course, if the party is somehow important to the story.

Which brings us to when it's okay to "tell, don't show." Telling advances the plot in a short period of time, which is almost always necessary during some part of your story. Instead of showing your character making a phone call and the back and forth dialogue of the phone call, then driving to the courthouse to file a form, and detailing those scenes, and having lunch with her mother, and showing what they eat and talk about, it's more expeditious and preferable to write, "She called Teddy to double-check the appointment, dropped by the courthouse to file necessary paperwork, then had lunch with her mom." If you don't tell *some* of the time, your story will be too tedious and you'll lose the reader.

Show the scenes in your book that are important to the plot or to the emotional growth of your character. *Tell* the scenes that are logistical or aren't crucial to the plot.

132. Using placeholders

You're typing along at top speed when suddenly you realize you don't know the name of that *thing* you meant to look up...or you can't remember the name of the town your heroine grew up in. Resist the urge to stop and do research or perform searches when you're in the groove of writing. Because a few seconds of research will lead to a few minutes, which can kill your momentum. When I'm writing and I realize I need a piece of information I don't have or can't recall, I type XXXXX and keep going. Later I search on X's to go back and fill in what I need.

133. Imagination drill!

A man with no money needs to get from point A to point B. Can you come up 10 different ways he can beg, borrow, or steal a ride in/on 10 different modes of transportation?

1.

2.

3.

4.

5.

6.

7.

8.

9.

10.

(For printable PDFs of all Imagination Drills, go to
www.stephaniebond.com.)

134. Overwriting

When I was in high school taking a second year art class, there was a senior student who was widely regarded as the most talented artist in the school. He set up his easel in our class and spent the entire semester painting an elaborate seascape to enter in the county-wide art exhibition for students. He used watercolors, acrylics, and oils, applying the paint with numerous brushes and palette knives. The rest of us, of course, were in awe of the painting and the amount of time he spent on it. The painting was much admired during the art exhibit, and everyone assumed this student would win not only first place in the painting category, but would likely win the Best in Show award. When the judges announced the winners, however, the painting was given a disappointing third place ribbon. Later I asked our art instructor why the painting hadn't fared better. He said, "The judges said it was overworked."

It was the first time I'd heard the term; my instructor explained it meant the student had worked on the painting, revising and adding and tweaking until all the energy, all the freshness of his original concept was gone. My instructor privately pointed out where the breaking waves were stiff and the layered colors were muddy. It was a good lesson for me—that the quality of a creative endeavor doesn't always correlate to the time spent creating it. Part of a good, creative instinct is knowing when to stop, and when to edit.

The same is true for writing—writers fall in love with their own words and thus, find it hard to move on. When we write a good line, it's compelling to want to prop it up with other good lines and maybe go back and write a better setup for the line. Or say it again in another sentence, but differently. It's easy to get caught in the trap of overwriting; take care your original idea isn't smothered or is simply lost in the sheer volume of words. Say it once and say it well, then move on.

135. Flashbacks

The flashback is an old device used to transport the reader to a scene from the past. Flashbacks were popular in commercial fiction of the 1970s and 1980s, but eventually fell out of vogue. A warning to new writers: Flashbacks can be a red flag that screams "beginner!" Flashbacks fell out of favor because they take the reader out of the current story, which is distracting and can seem tedious. If done cleverly, flashbacks can be effective, but ask yourself if a flashback is really necessary. For instance, instead of having a flashback scene where the heroine first meets the hero in high school, can you have her tell a friend about it? Or have a friend who was there remind her of it? You can have your character fondly remember an occasion without having a full flashback scene. Use flashbacks sparingly and only for effect.

136. Italics

Italics are used for emphasis, so a little goes a long way. For example, flashback scenes are typically written in italics, which is one of the reasons readers find them tedious. Dream sequences are also typically written in italics—which tips off the reader it's a dream and can lessen its effect—and, again, can be tedious. Other common applications for italics:

Words in dialogue and elsewhere that require emphasis:
"I *told* you it was going to blow!"
I opened my eyes and sighed. Today was my birthday. The *big* one.

Internal monologue:
Angie sat down hard in the chair. *What do I want?* She didn't know.

Remembered dialogue:
My mind raced as I tried to remember what Jim had said about the night Sandy was killed. *Sandy told me she was headed to the bar.*

Note: If you're writing a manuscript for submission to an editor, it's proper form to underline the text versus italicizing; underlining is easier for the line editor and copyeditor to see, and to correct if they disagree.

137. Cueing the reader

Part of a writer's job is cueing the reader as to what in the story is important, either by the way (and order) we introduce elements or by the amount of page we spend on it. For example, the simplest way to communicate, "Hey, reader, this is the main character!" is to introduce the main character first. If you choose to begin your story with a character other than the main character, you should be brief, and somehow cue the reader the story is moving toward the introduction of the main character. Once the main character is introduced, you should spend more page on that character than other characters, i.e., tell as many scenes from the main character's point of view as possible.

Conversely, don't devote as much space to elements that are secondary or extraneous to the story. Don't mention the character's intense claustrophobia unless it will come into play at some point. There's an old writing adage that goes something like "Don't put an antique gun over the fireplace mantle unless you're going to use it." As you grow your writing skillset, you'll find more and more ways to use cueing to your storytelling advantage.

138. Repetition

In the section on overwriting, I warned against diluting a strong thought through inadvertent repetition. Be on guard for repetition, whether it be in the form of word usage, character movements, scene venues, use of secondary characters, or even character names beginning with the same letter.

In one of my romantic comedies, *About Last Night*, I gave the heroine a sister who was her confidante. I was a few chapters into the manuscript when my editor called and said the publisher had received good reader response from one of my secondary characters (a gay man) in a previous book, and was it possible to work him into this book? It was; I made him an employee in the hotel where the story was set. But soon I realized the heroine was having a conversation with her sister, then having the same conversation with the new planted character. I realized both characters were filling the same role (confidante), so the sister had to go.

Repetition erodes your writing—writer beware.

139. Tangents—don't go there

If you're following a synopsis/chapter outline, you're going to be less tempted to go off on a story tangent. To writers who write by the seat of their pants, tangents are an entertaining diversion from the main plot. It's true that while following a tangent, you might stumble upon an amazing thread that will rescue or elevate your story. But more often than not, tangents will simply frustrate you, slow you down, and you'll end up with pages you'll have to scrap. And for the writers who say they're compelled to go off on a tangent, that it's where the story took them, I would respond *you* are the writer, *you* are in control of the story, not the other way around.

140. Balancing exposition and dialogue

An aspiring writer recently asked me how I know to balance exposition with dialogue. The truth is, I don't know. For me, it's all about pacing. If a character needs some "alone time" to digest something monumental, exposition and internal monologue slows things down. Dialogue picks up the pace again—as long as your characters don't make a speech. Long, flowing sentences carry the reader along. Short, staccato sentences are more action-oriented or emphatic. If you skipped the section on whitespace, this would be a good time to go back and read it.

As you write, if you remain aware of how everything works together to affect the delivery and the reading experience, you're more likely to strike a successful balance. The element of balance is one you will hone and refine the more you write—with each project, you'll develop better instincts for how best to tell that particular story.

YOUR WORK ARENA

An average performer can be elevated to greatness by
the atmosphere of where the game is played!

141. Commit to yourself

A lot of writers I know complain their friends and family don't take their writing seriously, and I contend it's probably because the writers don't take themselves seriously. The satisfaction you get out of your writing will be directly related to the commitment you make to your writing. That might mean sacrificing social time, writing when you don't feel like it, and even making new friends. (You'll soon discover no one understands a writer like another writer.) Your commitment is what will carry you through the tough times, when you feel as if you're not talented enough or not original enough, or not (fill in the blank) enough. A commitment is a step above a whim or a notion—it's the feeling you're being called to write a story, and making a promise to yourself to see it through to the end. I'm a big believer in writing down goals, so perhaps one of your first written sentences should be "I am committed to writing a novel." You'll be surprised how putting those simple words to paper (or to file) can be the impetus for writing enough words to complete an entire manuscript!

142. Enlist your family's support

Writing is a selfish endeavor. When you write, you can't really pay attention to anything or anyone else. Worse, to your family, it can seem like you're involved in a super fun and exciting adventure, and you're doing it without them. Even if your family is supportive in the beginning, resentment might begin to creep in after a while, especially if your writing time intrudes on family time. I cannot stress how important it is that you enlist and sustain your family's support for your writing. Writing is hard enough, so if on top of writing, you get grief for doing it, you won't be doing it for long.

The best way to recruit supporters within your household is to play "What if" games with them and engage them in the plotting and planning of the book, or in the more visual elements, such as creating a collage for your story, or creating a mockup of your cover. You can also make your family your research assistants to help you track down details for your story. And you might ask family and friends to read scenes and get their feedback on how a man/woman/teenager/grandparent would talk or react.

Writing a novel is a solitary undertaking, but it doesn't have to be isolating. Involving your friends and family in the process is a terrific way to get them invested in your goals.

143. Your work space

Your home-base work space is important because it will set the tone for how seriously you take yourself and how seriously other people take you. Your home office could be a corner of a room, a hallway, the landing on the stairs, the garage, the attic, the basement, the spare bedroom, or the spare bathroom, but it should be a space dedicated to your writing files and equipment, a space you can access anytime (and ideally, a space off-limits to others).

And bigger isn't always better. I'm reminded of a writer who said in an interview she was delighted with the financial success of her first book—it allowed her to move to a bigger apartment with a roomy office. But it wasn't long before she realized having all that space around her and a view was so distracting, she couldn't write! She wound up setting a chair and TV tray table in a closet and writing there instead—she said opening the door to the closet was akin to opening a door onto her story. A smaller space worked for her.

My dedicated writing spaces have varied in size and amenities. The most productive phase of my career was spent sitting in front of a rolling laptop cart in a tiny space in a shared office. Experiment to see what works best for you.

144. How to decorate your office space

I use the word "decorate" lightly because your work space doesn't have to be designer-inspired; in fact, some writers might find writing in a dressed-up space to be too intimidating, as if the writing has to measure up to the surroundings! But it pays to put some thought into making your work area clean, functional, and friendly. Finding (and making) time to write is hard enough—don't make it even harder on yourself by having a work area you avoid because bills, laundry, or toys are overflowing the area. And try to incorporate details to stimulate your senses: plants, a sound machine, a scented candle, a heated chair cushion, and a coaster for your favorite beverage.

145. Change of venue

If you have the run of your house, don't be afraid to change up where you write. I typically write at my desk, but if I'm feeling restless, I will work at my kitchen bar, or in my bedroom. In fact, one way I can get in an extra few pages a day is to put my laptop next to my bed and when I wake up, write while my mind is freshly recharged. Another advantage of my bedroom is because there are no windows, it feels insular and cozy and makes me feel "close" to the work.

Changing work venues gives me a different point of view—literally. When I was a coder in the corporate world and I ran into a problem in a program I was writing or decoding, I would sometimes move to my guest chair, or even the opposite side of my desk to force my brain to look at things from another angle—and it always worked. Simply changing your work environment can jumpstart your brain out of complacency.

146. Writing in public places

Although most writers have abandoned pen and paper, the age-old allure of writing in a coffee shop or diner remains. It can be inspiring to plant yourself in the middle of a bustling scene. Bookstores are perennial favorite places for writers to get inspired, although those venues are on the verge of extinction. Wine shops, cigar bars, and mall food courts offer their own atmosphere.

At different times in my career, I've belonged to co-working spaces where I pay a fee to have access to the public work rooms with wi-fi and coffee stations, plus the ability to reserve a private workroom. Co-working spaces usually have a cool vibe and are frequented by freelancers in every industry. If you're an aspiring writer, check out local hangouts for environments that motivate you. Some things to look for: roomy chairs and/or tables, an outlet for your devices, food and/or drink you like, and a generally good atmosphere, such as friendly staff and good background music.

147. Writing anywhere

At different times in the process of finishing your novel, you might need to get creative about finding a place to write or figuring out how to write wherever you happen to be. Sometimes I like to work outside, either at my home, or at the park, etc. The problem with working outside on a backlit laptop is seeing the screen in the sunlight. My solution is to wear a cap with a long bill, like the kind you'd wear on the beach. Just having your eyes shaded will help you better see the computer screen.

Keep a to-go bag handy with items to help you write away from your home office: a copy of your synopsis/outline, pad of paper, pen, a portable charger, eye drops, etc. I do much of my writing on the train, in airports, on planes, and in waiting rooms.

In an effort to combine writing with a walking workout, I've found a way to write on the treadmill at the gym. I cut a piece of foam core board the depth of my laptop, and long enough to span the handrails of the treadmill. The board acts as a work surface and positions the keyboard at a good height for me to type. I can walk about 3mph and comfortably keep my hands on the keyboard. I walk for an hour and usually come away with 3-4 new pages. I call it "wrilking." (Note: *Do not* try wrilking unless you're a touch typist and relatively coordinated! And if you do try this at home or at the gym, please be careful and start at a very slow speed.)

Learning to write in any environment will help you eke pages out of what would otherwise be "down" time.

148. What time of day to write

I can get so much writing done early in the morning before my phone starts singing and my email starts dinging. Ditto for the hours between 8:00 pm and midnight—no doorbell ringing, no email pinging, no errands to run. And now that shows can be watched anytime, no appointment TV to distract.

So, I generally like to write early in the day and late in the day. But when I'm nearing the end of a manuscript, my writing hours become progressively more peculiar. I stay up until 2:00 am, then 3:00 am, then 4:00 am writing. When I'm near the end, there's no use going to bed earlier because I simply lie awake thinking about the manuscript. So I wait until 1) I forget the main characters' names, 2) my fingers are so tired I'm typing with my knuckles, or 3) my forehead slams down on the keyboard. Then I catch a few Zzzzs, and get back to it the next morning. I can feel the momentum growing as the day wears on, and sure enough, when the sun sets, my creative juices really start cooking.

Every writer has a different time of the day they prefer to write, and that might change as you work through different parts of the manuscript. Listen to your body's rhythm and write when you have the most creative energy. Then if you get a chance to squeeze in writing at other times during the day, it'll be bonus work.

149. Display Tricks

If you spend a lot of time looking at your computer, play with combinations of bright-to-dim overhead lights and bright-to-dim lighting on your laptop screen. (The keys to adjust the monitor lighting are typically on the keyboard.) FYI, not only does your computer leave the factory with the monitor brightness set too high, but the contrast is probably set too low. Remember to adjust the brightness as the lighting in the room changes at different times of the day.

Another way to give your eyes a break is to adjust your display to something above 100%. I write in a regular 12-point font, but I increase the display to 120% for easier viewing. You can also increase the font size itself.

A writing friend of mine uses a large TV screen as her monitor while she operates the keyboard from a recliner. She says it motivates her to see her words scrolling across a big screen. Experiment with display modes and lighting to enhance your writing environment.

150. Listening to music while you write

Music is a sensory detail I introduce into my work environment when I need to get some good pages written. It keeps me stimulated on a subconscious level. I mostly listen to music channels on television or through online radio stations, and I look for something that's going to get me in the mood to write about particular characters, places, or scenes: nostalgic tunes, love songs, holiday music, etc. I prefer not to listen to music with earphones while I write because it feels a little too intrusive for me. On the few occasions when I do wear earbuds, I listen to music in a language I don't understand so I'm not distracted by the lyrics.

Check out the exhaustive list of music channels available to you and try to imagine a scene, character, or setting in a book each type of music conjures up.

151. Creating a playlist for your book

Another way to establish a sensory environment to write by is to create a musical playlist for your book. The playlist might be made up of songs that have to do with the plot or the mood of the book, or it could be a list of songs your main character might listen to. You can compare a playlist for your book to the soundtrack for a movie—think of how music intensifies the emotion or action happening onscreen. Creating a playlist will help you get your head into your book...and it's a fun item to share with readers or potential readers while you're working on your novel, and afterward, while you're promoting it. (Just take care not to infer the singer/writer of the song endorses your book.)

TIME OUT!

Remember, there's no specific way, special place, or certain time you should write. I'm giving you lots of examples and choices to experiment with. Adopt the strategy that's most productive for you, and when you find yourself in a rut, change up the game plan!

152. The myth of muse

The Muse(s) are nine goddesses of inspiration for the arts and sciences, sometimes collectively referred to as Muse. Some creatives cite people as their Muse—perhaps a love interest or another person who inspires them to greatness. That's really sweet.

And it's total hooey. Because the implication is if you don't have a Muse, you have to wait for one, i.e., wait for inspiration to strike—like lightning. In my opinion, when writers talk about Muse/inspiration, it's just a procrastination tactic. Because Muse is too unreliable for a working writer to count on.

The better technique is simply to "force it." Force yourself to sit still long enough to get something down on paper/the screen, and force the elements of your story to work together. If they don't want to, make them. If they misbehave, get them in line. I can't count the times I've dropped a plot point into my synopsis I know I need, sometimes with no idea how I'm going to get there—yet. But if I keep massaging the synopsis, I always, always, *always*, find a way to make it all work.

Remember, you are driving the bus here, not Muse. And the funny thing is, the harder you work on your story, the more likely Muse will pay you a visit.

153. Writing Rituals

I'm often asked if I have any writing rituals—a legitimate question since many writers are superstitious creatures. I'm not superstitious, but I'm a bit of a control freak, and the two are scarily similar.

I like for my office and writing setup to be a certain way. I like for specific things to be within reach—reference books, pens and paper, my short- and long-term to-do lists. I like to set my background noise to business news or a music channel. I like to read three or four favorite blogs/websites before I begin to write. I like to read the last paragraph I wrote during my previous writing stint to get me back into the story.

I know some writers who can't write if there's any background noise at all. And some who can't write unless their pet is curled up near their feet. And some who can't write if it's too hot or too cold or their horoscope says to stay in bed.

Every writer will develop their own little routine that best gets them psyched up to write—meditation? A cup of tea in a favorite mug? But don't let rituals take up too much time or become a necessary part of your writing to the point that they impede your progress.

154. Typical writing day

Another question I'm often asked is about my daily schedule—how much time do I spend writing versus doing other things, like paperwork, laundry, and having fun? The time I spend writing usually depends on how pressing my deadlines are and how fast the pages are accumulating. For instance, rather than saying I'm going to write six hours today, I might say I'm going to write 10 pages; if it takes me two hours to write them, great. If it takes me ten hours to write them, then so be it. Regardless, I usually put in a 10-hour day on my writing career, six days a week. If I'm not writing, I'm answering correspondence, working on my website, doing promotional activities, or dealing with the paperwork required to keep my business running. Being a full-time writer is like running any business—there's always something to do. Some tasks are more urgent than others, and priorities can change with a phone call or a delivery. For a working writer, there's no such thing as a typical writing day. It's all a balancing act. But...

Best. Job. Ever.

155. Scheduling writing time

I've included several sections already on when to write and where to write, but the overall message is it's important to find a way to write regularly. One of the worst habits a writer can get into is waiting for a long, uninterrupted block of time to write. It simply won't happen, or at least not often enough to finish writing a novel. Most of my books have been completed in 30-minute increments here, 15-minute increments there. A continuous hour of writing is a luxury. Two hours? Unheard of. So it's best if you learn how to immerse yourself into your story quickly and how to get things done in a short period of time. I also parse out writing "tasks" depending on how much time I have in that sitting. I might write, or I might decide to edit what I wrote earlier, or I might work on the plot, or do research.

The good news? With dogged determination and a firm goal, you can accomplish a lot in stolen slices of time over a day/week/month/year.

156. A writing habit

Whatever you have accomplished up to now and the general state of your life is due to a series of habits: Your general health is due to your habits of diet and exercise. Your level of education is due to your habits of study and self-discipline. Your proficiency at hobbies like playing a musical instrument or golf is due to your habits of practice and execution. Likewise, your ability to finish a novel is due to the writing habits you develop. If you adopt a "do it" attitude about writing regularly, like brushing your teeth, without assigning emotional baggage/fallout to the task, you can't help but be productive.

157. Should you share your dreams?

I mentioned earlier how to get your family invested in your writing for the good of all parties. So, it's up to you, but I do believe the people living in your home should be let in on the good news you're writing a novel.

But outside your home, maybe not. If, for example, you have a full-time job, your employer might consider writing a novel as moonlighting, which could jeopardize your main source of income. And if your coworkers know you're writing a book, your time at work might be scrutinized more closely if someone worries you'll work on your novel on company time. In general, it's probably not a good idea to plant the seed in your boss's head that your concentration and loyalties are divided. And if you work in a sensitive industry (law, intelligence, government, finance, medicine), you don't want associates suspecting you might be blowing the whistle on private business transactions.

When it comes to sharing your writing aspirations with acquaintances, do it if you believe the person will be supportive and/or if it makes you feel more accountable and more apt to finish your novel. But consider the consequences.

158. Imagination drill!

A woman runs into the bathroom to throw up. Can you come up with 10 explanations?

1.

2.

3.

4.

5.

6.

7.

8.

9.

10.

(For printable PDFs of all Imagination Drills, go to
www.stephaniebond.com.)

159. Don't quit your day job

Lots of aspiring writers dream of quitting their day job to write. If you have a day job, please don't quit...at least not at first. The idea that you can get more writing done without a day job is a myth—some of my most productive years were when I was working full-time and later, part-time at my corporate job. Having a limited amount of time to write meant I had to be ultra-productive, so I was. And the money for a novel, if you're lucky enough to sell it, can be looooooooooooong in coming. The submission process takes a long time, and if you get an offer, contracts take seemingly forever to negotiate and be processed, then it will be months or maybe a year or more before the book is released, and royalties are even farther down the road. If you self-publish, the money will be more immediate, but the amount will be unpredictable and unreliable. Good decisions are rarely made from a position of poverty. Don't put that kind of pressure on yourself, and don't think that committing to a writing career means dropping all other work obligations. You will be more creative and productive if you're not worried about making ends meet.

160. Finding time to write when you have a full-time job

If you have a full-time job, how are you supposed to find time to write, especially if you have a family or other obligations in the evenings and on the weekends?

I'm glad you asked! If you have a full-time job and other commitments in the evening, do what I did: Grab writing time on your commute and during your lunch hour or breaks. If you drive to and from work, consider dictating into a recorder and transcribing the notes later. Or maybe this is the time to join a carpool or opt for public transportation so you'll spend less time driving, more time writing.

I also made it a practice to write on my lunch hour away from my office. Sometimes I could steal away to another floor of the building where I worked, or to a vending area, cafeteria, or nearby café. And sometimes I took my laptop to my car and wrote there. (Hey, I really wanted to be a novelist!)

Writers have to be resourceful. If you analyze your daily work schedule, I'll bet you'll find some underutilized time you can take back for writing.

161. Carving out time to write

In order to find time to write, you have to have the time available in the first place. To get your novel written, you might have to cut back on favors and volunteer work. This is especially true if you don't have a job outside the home or are retired. If you're every friend, neighbor and relative's "go-to" person for concierge services, know it will take some time to retrain everyone. (People generally are irritated when you won't make their life easier.) And you're going to have to give up the warm, fuzzy feeling of always saving the day. The next time someone asks you to do something that will infringe on your writing time, just say, "Sorry, I can't—I have an appointment." No one has to know it's an appointment with your laptop.

162. Protecting your writing time

When it comes to getting your writing done, there's no single more important element than protecting your time. When you work at home, you tend to get those calls from various friends and relatives during the day because the perception is you're not *really* working and, in fact, will welcome an excuse to take a break. Email also intrudes, and the doorbell...and other people who live in your home. To protect your writing time:

Eliminate electronic interruptions. Turn off your phone ringer and your email/social media notification. Unless you're on an organ transplant waiting list, nothing is so important it can't wait a few minutes.

Employ "do not disturb" signals. A sign works, but also a closed door or headphones. A writing friend with children has trained them to not interrupt her when she's wearing the red sweater; the green sweater means it's okay.

Remove yourself. Instead of complaining people don't respect your space/time, remove yourself to a private place.

163. The physical demands of writing

Writers spend long hours with their arms, hands, and neck in unnatural positions. And new studies suggest sitting is the new smoking, i.e., will lead to lots of health issues. To stave off a host of physical problems, maintain good posture and invest in a good chair. (If you're avoiding your home office space, it might be a sign it's not conducive to working comfortably.) A balance ball desk chair is a good way to work your core muscles while you sit. Pay attention to pains in your neck, back, shoulders, arms, and hands; take breaks every thirty minutes or so to realign everything. I keep a yoga mat on the floor near my desk so I can stretch and do energizing exercises. And I sometimes put my laptop on the breakfast bar and stand at my computer to work. Also, regular neck and shoulder massages aren't a luxury for writers, but a necessity. As with any job, it's important to know the cumulative physical effects of writing and to do everything you can to stay healthy.

164. The mental demands of writing

I'm not sure if writers are prone to dark moods, or if people with dark moods are attracted to the writing profession. Most writers are introverts, so that already puts us behind the sociable bell curve. And most writers sit down to the computer with some baggage, i.e., insecurities that what we're writing isn't good enough. Some writers feel compelled to write *because* of an unhappy childhood or other experience.

Whew...we can be a morose bunch!

It's natural to have some reservations about the work, about letting other people read it, about revising when we don't want to, about unflattering feedback, rejection, and bad reviews. Top it off with the fact that writing is such a solitary experience, and it's easy to turn inward and let those doubts multiply. Anxieties can manifest in bad writer behavior—pouting, lashing out, jealousy, anger, or shutting down. Writing is a personal journey, but you don't have to take every reaction to your work so personally, and you don't have to play out the stereotype that writing a novel is a long-suffering, angst-ridden endeavor.

Writing might seem like a passive, soft, or even easy vocation, but the truth is, fiction-writing isn't for sissies. You have to develop a thick skin and unshakable confidence—not in the belief that everything you create will always be right, but in the belief you'll always be able to revise and make it right, or your next attempt will be better. Writing a novel can be a mentally draining process because you put so much of yourself into it. But keep things in perspective—writing a novel should be a positive, happy, enriching experience!

165. Blank Screen Syndrome

In the design competition show *Project Runway*, budding clothing designers are given challenges with specific constraints of what they can and can't do, typically around a theme. Some designers thrive under the challenges, some don't. But what's interesting to me is to see how the tables are flipped when the contestants are given free rein to create anything they want, as long as it expresses their design aesthetic. Without constraints, some designers fall apart. When presented with all the possibilities, they simply can't make a decision and their resulting garment is a mess.

Similarly, sitting down to write without any constraints can lead to Blank Screen Syndrome. You put your hands on the keyboard, but nothing happens. The screen gapes back at you, empty...expectant...accusatory. Blank Screen Syndrome can be paralyzing, and stop a good novel in its tracks. Blank Screen Syndrome is an epidemic in the writing world, and needs to be eradicated. Here are some ways you can inoculate yourself against Blank Screen Syndrome:

- Do your thinking away from the computer. When you're in front of your laptop, you should be typing.
- If you're stuck, get up and walk away for a few minutes, then come back to your computer when you're ready to start typing.
- Stop writing in the middle of a dialogue exchange, or in a spot where you know what happens next. That way when you sit down to write, you can hit the ground running.

166. Dressing the part

Since we were just talking about clothes, now might be a good time to talk about dressing the part of a writer. I'm not talking about what to wear to your first booksigning—hey, go crazy on that day. But when you're writing, sometimes what you wear can make a difference in how you work.

You should always dress comfortably, and I confess there have been deadline days when I didn't change out of my pajamas, although I don't recommend it as a regular practice. Wearing your p.j.'s all day can make you feel as if you're not part of the real world, and that writing isn't a legitimate pastime. Plus, the UPS guys will dread ringing your doorbell.

Since I write full-time, I generally put on workout gear and good sneakers every morning so I can stand to work at my computer, and take a break to go to the gym sometime during the day. But there are times when I deviate.

If I go out in public to write, say to a co-working space, I dress business casual (or at least a jacket over jeans) because I don't want to look like a slob and I never know when I might meet a potential business associate. And a couple of times after finishing projects back to back and feeling burnt out, I was finding it hard to get back in the swing of things. So for a week I dressed to go downstairs to my home office as if I were commuting to a corporate office in a high-rise...and it worked to get me back on track!

IN THE HUDDLE

There are forces all around to help you achieve your goals!

167. It takes a village

You don't have to go it alone as a writer. In fact, I suggest you don't. Writing can be a very solitary and isolating activity. Joining writing organizations and networking with other writers can be good for your mental health and your career. Your skillset will grow faster, and being around people who are like-minded will keep you going when motivation drags.

Most national writing organizations are genre specific, and have state or local chapters so you can attend meetings and conferences. A quick check on the Internet or at your local library will yield the names of writing groups. Some are open to all writers, some expect you to pursue writing in their targeted genre, some require publication before joining. My advice is to attend a meeting of all the groups in your area to decide when one best fits your needs. If you can't find a group in your area, you can connect with writers online. Most organizations offer outreach chapters that meet online for members who don't have a "home" chapter.

At worst, you'll be out the time it takes to check out the writing groups. At best, you'll forge friendships that will last a lifetime.

168. Seeking feedback

New writers I've talked to express apprehension (even terror) at the thought of letting a relative stranger read their work. I understand completely—it takes guts to make yourself vulnerable and put your work out there for possible annihilation. You've spent months, maybe years, working on this manuscript—it's your baby. The last thing you want is for someone to tell you your baby is ugly!

Feedback, criticism, and rejection are all part of the writing business—but fortunately, so is *good* feedback and acceptance. It might help to tell yourself when you receive criticism on your manuscript that it's not personal...except to you. Almost without exception, feedback is meant to help you make your manuscript as strong as possible, and isn't that what you want—the opportunity to make your book as good as it can be?

169. Critique groups

Unless your spouse or mother is an editor, they are not the most reliable source for feedback on your manuscript. Everyone I meet who wants to write a book asks me for the secret handshake—you know, the *one* sure way to publication, so (drumroll, please) HERE IT IS:

Join a critique group.

A critique group is a group of writers who exchange work regularly and provide feedback. I've been a member of a critique group for the entirety of my career—before I was published and now still, seventy-plus books later. I credit critique groups with helping me find focus, keeping my production on track, and staying sane in a crazy business.

In my opinion, the most effective critique groups:

- Have no more than four members
- Establish rules and expectations for members
- Meet once a week
- Meet at a public place, away from the distractions of work and home
- Are made up of members with similar goals: Is everyone writing part-time around another job or family? Is publication the end game?

Even veteran, multi-published authors will benefit greatly from being in a critique group—do it. DO IT.

170. Forming a critique group

If you can't find a critique group to join, consider forming one of your own. Ask other writers you know, or make an announcement at your next writers meeting.

To keep everything light and friendly, you might suggest forming a *temporary* critique group to prepare for a contest or other goal. During this exercise, everyone's objectives, work ethic, production schedule, and writing ability will become apparent. At the end of the time period, the group will disband, as previously agreed. But if you clicked with one or more of the writers who seem to have similar goals, ask them if they'd like to start meeting regularly to critique.

Please don't fall into the emotional trap of asking someone to join a critique group because you don't want them to feel left out or because you feel sorry for them. Trust me, it'll only be worse in the long run.

And this might be a good time to ask yourself if *you* are serious enough and thick-skinned enough to be a good critique partner. Do you need to recommit to your writing first?

A good critique group is like a chorus—sometimes you have to experiment with different members to get the harmony just right. My critique groups went through periods of contraction and expansion as members fell away or were invited to join based on the dynamics of the group. A bad critique group is worse than none. But a great one will advance your writing career by leaps and bounds.

171. Brainstorming with others

My brother works in the hotel business and is always calling to tell me about encounters with nutty people. It's not uncommon for us to be talking and for him to suddenly say, "Gotta go—there's a naked guy in the lobby." I set a romantic comedy (*Naughty or Nice?*) in a hotel and featured antics inspired by some of his hair-raising tales of working with the public.

When he moved from San Francisco to Manhattan a few years ago, we talked about his trials of relocating. When he found an apartment, he called the movers to deliver his stored furniture. Then he said, "Now I just hope when the delivery arrives, it's my stuff!" That's when my writer's brain kicked in. "Oh, but it would be more fun if they delivered someone else's stuff." Then my brother said, "And the stuff they delivered was nicer than my stuff, so I decided to keep it." Then I said, "And you discover later the person living down the hall got your stuff and decided to keep it." We went on and on, developing a relationship between these two people who fell in love with someone else's stuff. It was fun and who knows—I just might use it in a book someday.

The moral of the story is it's nice to have someone to brainstorm with! There's something about vocalizing your ideas, bouncing them off a live person, that gets your creativity jumping!

172. Collaborating with another writer

There are advantages to writing with a partner—you can match strengths and weaknesses. And if you're the kind of writer who has a problem with self-discipline, working with a partner can help to keep you on track. And if there are two of you, you can divvy up expenses and promotional activities. But there are also disadvantages to writing with a partner—what name will you use? What happens if you disagree on how a project should proceed? What if one of you has a disagreement with your agent or your editor? What if one of you wants to write side projects on your own? What if one of you has a personal emergency or illness when a deadline needs to be met? And then there's the reality of having to split income. A writing partnership can test a friendship.

If you decide to collaborate with someone on a writing project, you are literally choosing to go into business with that person; it makes sense to talk about guidelines and put them in writing, for both of you, and for your heirs. A writing partnership can be successful as long as each party goes in with a clear understanding of how the partnership will unfold—in good times and bad.

173. Contests

Most national writing organizations and some publishing houses sponsor contests for unpublished authors. Some contests are thematic, such as Best Opening Scene, or Best Love Scene, or even Best Synopsis. Writing contests can be helpful, but check out the particulars before you enter:

- Is there a category in which your story would fit?
- Is there an entry fee and does it seem reasonable?
- Who is judging the entries—published authors in your field? Editors?
- What kind of feedback will you receive—a written critique, or simply a score, and will you receive the feedback in a timely manner?
- What are the prizes? (Can range from certificates to cash awards to getting your work in front of an editor.)

Contests can be helpful in terms of letting you know if your work is ready to submit to an editor, and have given more than one writer the opportunity they needed to become published. But there are some pitfalls to entering contests:

- Don't try to rework your story just to "fit" a category in a contest.
- The feedback you receive might not be correct, or relevant to your goals.
- Don't get caught in the trap of rewriting and polishing an entry-length project (such as the synopsis and first chapter) and entering it into contest after contest without moving forward to finish the manuscript.

Writing magazines and websites list writing contests; universities and libraries are other good sources for contests. Regardless of the source, read the terms and conditions carefully. When you enter material into a contest, you might be signing away or restricting rights to your entry. Utilize contests as a productivity tool, not an end goal.

STAY IN THE GAME

It's not enough to sit on the sidelines—you have to put in playing time to rack up some stats!

174. Page production—how much should you be writing?

I'm not sure anything causes as much anxiety for writers as wondering and worrying about how much (in pages) they should be writing, as if there's a minimum threshold of words to be written before you can legitimately call yourself a novelist.

There isn't a minimum threshold, but it's good to be able to estimate and measure page production: A full manuscript page (double-spaced, 12-point font) is approximately 250 words. A full-length novel comes in between 80,000 and 100,000 words, which is 320-400 pages.

So the average full-length novel is about 350 manuscript pages. If, as I mentioned in the beginning of this book, you write one manuscript page for every tip in this book (365), you'll have a full manuscript at the end. So, if you write one manuscript page per day, at the end of one year, you'll have written one book. If you write two manuscript pages per day, at the end of one year, you'll have written two books. And so on.

Is it starting to sound doable?

I have a writing friend who has trained herself to write 5 pages in one hour, every morning from 7:00 - 8:00 am. And sure enough, she publishes about 5 books every year. Sound impossible? Do the math.

I'm not saying you should be producing 5 pages a day every day, but it's good to know what's possible, and push yourself when you have the opportunity.

175. More on page production

Instead of focusing on daily production, I've found it more productive to concentrate on a weekly page production goal. A weekly goal is more realistic with my erratic schedule that requires me to spend a lot of time on non-writing activities.

I use a plain old monthly desk calendar to help me keep track of my weekly page production, but you can use an electronic prompt, or whatever works for you.

Let's say my weekly page production goal is 25 pages. On Monday I write 3 pages, so at the end of day I make a notation on the calendar of cumulative pages written versus my page goal: 3/25. On Tuesday, I write 2 pages, so the notation is 5/25. On Wednesday, I write 1 page, so I'm at 6/25, and starting to feel the pressure. Thursday I write 6 pages, so 12/25. Friday I write 5 pages, so 17/25. Saturday I write 4 pages, so 21/25, and Sunday I write 2 pages, which means I fell a little short at 23/25. BUT I know I probably wrote more pages than I would have if I hadn't set a goal for myself.

Sunday evening I take a look at my schedule for the week ahead, and set another weekly goal.

176. Should you write every day?

I personally believe it's important to write every day, including Sunday, even if it's only a paragraph or two. Not only is it good to develop a writing habit, like brushing your teeth, but I think I'm driven by the fear that what's in my head today won't be there tomorrow, and I'll never be able to think of that one thing again. (Borne out by the fact that when I read something I wrote a few months ago, not only do I have no recollection of writing it, but I think, *Wow…that's not bad and I'm glad I wrote it down at the time, because I'm not sure I could think of it again.*)

Some people have objections to writing on the weekends for familial or religious reasons, which is understandable. Aside from your personal beliefs on the matter, the best way to decide if you would benefit from writing on the weekend is to scrutinize your work habits on Monday: Are you raring to go after one or two days away from your computer, ready to dive back into your story? Or do you piddle and procrastinate because the one or two days away have interrupted your momentum?

177. Writing fast, writing well

Every writer has to find a writing pace they're comfortable with, but I challenge the myth that people who write fast cannot also write well. People who write fast and well typically are the type of writers who have the characters and story worked out in their head, so they spend less time meandering off on tangents and having to scrap pages later. The advice to "take your time, let the story evolve" is valid if it suits your writing style, but don't use it as an excuse to eke out only a page every couple of days.

How do you know whether slow is your style or your excuse? Ask yourself: Does writing slow leave you frustrated with your overall progress? Does it make you approach your writing with less enthusiasm? Do you quickly lose interest in your work-in-progress? If so, then kick up your production a notch. For me, the longer it takes for me to write a novel, the longer it takes for me to write a novel. I'd rather push through it while my enthusiasm is high.

178. Little wins

Earlier in this book, I encouraged you to target your novel toward an established audience. My suggestion isn't rooted in a secret desire to mold you into a homogenous writer. Rather, my suggestion is rooted in a secret desire to see you win, i.e., experience success. The best way to stay motivated in any endeavor is to win early and win often; with this concept in mind, set up your writing goals so you can experience little wins along the way to the big win of completing your novel. Little wins can be thumping through a synopsis, or completing a scene or a chapter, or writing a really great dialogue exchange. Little wins might go unnoticed by others, but little wins are your own private glory.

179. Writer's block

Writer's Block is another one of those phrases writers like to toss around that makes them sound "writerly." Don't get me wrong—I believe Writer's Block exists; I just don't believe it's foisted onto a writer like the flu. If a writer is "blocked" from writing, there's a reason (of their own making):

a)   The character(s) is/are wrong.
b)   The plot has holes.
c)   The story isn't that interesting after all.
d)   The writer has gotten lazy.
e)   Any combination of the above.

Something has affected your enthusiasm for the story—what is it? Figure it out and fix it—that's what writers *do*. For working writers, Writer's Block is simply a caution flag, not a stop sign.

180. Bankable pages

I have a mantra for my writing: my goal is to write only bankable pages—pages that will sell. I don't like going on tangents and later scrapping pages—that's akin to scrapping money. Writing is hard enough; I don't want to see those precious pages piling up in the trash.

I'm exaggerating a bit because I haven't sold every single page I've ever written, but keeping the mantra of "bankable pages" in my mind has helped me to stay focused on how tightly a manuscript should be woven, and similarly, how cohesive my body of work should be.

181. When life interferes

Life happens. You're bumping along on your novel and you're on track to meet your deadline (either editor-directed or self-imposed). And then a family emergency occurs. Or a natural disaster. Or you're incapacitated in some way. You're definitely not going to meet your deadline, and in fact, you're not sure when you'll get back to writing at all. What should you do?

Take a deep breath. Every writer has to step away from a project at some point. The problem is even full-time novelists don't have paid sick days and vacation to take to deal with emergencies.

During a crisis, if you can squeeze in time to write even a paragraph here and there, you will be glad you did. But if mentally or physically you can't write, reading is the next best thing—read either pages you've written or something to keep you inspired. If neither is possible, you simply have to wait it out and just get back to your manuscript as soon as possible. The longer a manuscript sits, the colder it becomes and the harder it is to get your head back into it. But don't let a break from writing make a stressful situation even more stressful; your writing will be waiting for you when you're ready to get back to it. Writing is awesome that way.

182. Regaining momentum

I have a friend who took a hiatus from her writing career to nurse a terminally ill relative and grieve their passing. Afterward, she expressed desire to get back to writing because she knew how cathartic it could be for her, but she also harbored dread going back to unfinished projects left hanging in limbo and frankly, of picking up where she left off, as if nothing had happened.

Depending on the reason for and the length of your hiatus from writing, you might need to return to it with a new approach. If a lot of time has passed, you might find the projects you left unfinished don't have the same appeal or meaning as before. That's okay. (Although I warn you again discarding a project entirely—just move it to the back burner and revisit it at another time.)

To ease back into writing, read, read, read! And since you were writing before, you know the only way to get back to it is to *get back to it*. Hopefully you will bring a new sense of gratitude to your writing from the forced time away. No matter what's going on in my life, my writing has always been my salvation—it can be the same for you.

183. Imagination drill!

A woman picks up a weapon to defend herself. Describe the weapon and the situation if the scene is in:

A romantic comedy
A contemporary drama
A vampire story
A historical romance
A futuristic adventure
A suspense thriller
A horror novel
A fantasy tale
A cozy mystery
A faction novel set in 1942

(For printable PDFs of all Imagination Drills, go to
www.stephaniebond.com.)

184. Working on more than one project

It's best if you work on one project at a time and take an idea to completion before starting another one. But there might be times when you're working on more than one idea at a time. For example, if you take the first couple of chapters of an idea to your critique group to read, and you decide to flesh out another idea until you get their feedback on the first idea. Or you might be weighing two ideas and write a few chapters of each to see which one is stronger. Working writers often juggle many projects at once while they're each in different stages of the production lifecycle. If I have several projects on my desk, I try to give each of them part of my day, prioritizing them in terms of how much brain power they require. I might work on one in the morning, another one in the afternoon, and a different one in the evening. Or work on one project during the week, and another one on the weekends. Giving each project a little time means postponing the completion of each one, but it keeps me fresh, and makes me feel as if I'm making progress on each item. I keep chipping away at all of them and at some point, each project will reach a point of momentum, and then I'll finish it.

I'm often asked how I keep from getting my projects mixed up, but I find it similar to having breakfast with one group of people, lunch with another group of people, and dinner with another group of people!

185. Page sprinting

When I need to jumpstart my writing, I reach for my kitchen timer. I have an inexpensive model, the kind that clicks loudly as it winds down. I set it for 30 minutes, and see how much writing I can get done before the bell rings. Without fail, it always gets me going. Working under the gun adds an element of immediacy to any task, and gets your adrenaline going. Plus it's fun!

186. Constructive competition

Writers are usually a helpful, inspirational group. Use the power of a partner or a group to motivate you. Constructive, friendly competition for a short period of time might help you out of a rut. Ask around to find another writer who'd like to embark on an ambitious production goal, then check in often to help each other get there. My writing friends and I still have daily or weekly page challenges when we need to boost our production to meet a goal.

187. Destructive competition

Warning: Once you begin writing a novel, you will suddenly realize how many other people are writing or have written a novel. It's natural to compare your work/progress/sales to other writers, but don't let self-doubt or professional jealousy get the better of you—there's just no upside to feeling resentful of someone else's success or feeling as if they got your "place." There's enough shelf space for all our books now. There will always be someone doing "better" than you...and remember, there will always be someone looking at *you* and wishing they could have your talent/determination/ whatever.

188. The sagging middle

When aspiring writers envision the story they want to write, they generally have in their head how it will begin and how it will end. It's the middle that most writers cheerfully ignore—until they reach it. Even if you're working from an outline, the middle can get muddy and start to drag. Writers call this the sagging middle, which brings to mind the dragging belly of a sway-backed horse. The middle is where 1) you're getting into the thick of the plot, so you're dealing with details and logistics of conveying information to reader, so it can feel heavy and boring. Or 2) you know something more should be happening, but you're not sure how to get from point A to point B, so everything feels thin and wispy.

If you've reached a saggy part of the story and want to snag the reader's attention again, I recommend employing one of the 4 K's—kiss someone, kick someone, canoodle someone, or kill someone. Note that all of the 4 K's (okay, one "c") involve two characters, so in addition to shaking up the plot, shifting emotions will also come into play. A plot point that does double duty can't help but pick up the pace again.

REGROUP AND REBOUND

Every strategy has to be tweaked and fine-tuned in order to advance!

189. Self-editing

I believe it was my third manuscript that made me get serious about self-editing. I'd already sold two books to my publisher, and they wanted another one. I was starting to think about someday leaving my corporate job to write full-time, but after going through the protracted cycle of writing a manuscript and sending it in, waiting for revision notes, revising, then sending it back and waiting again for my editor to read it, perhaps give me more notes, etc., I started to realize I would never be able to publish enough books to make a living if I didn't find a way to streamline the process. And the part I could control was how clean and tight my manuscript was when I sent it in. So I started reading everything I could on self-editing and made a list of my weaknesses and things to be on the lookout for.

I also set up a system with my editor for her to read pages as we went along. I'd send her the first few chapters, she'd read them and give me feedback, I'd incorporate it and then send her more chapters, with a quick overview/reminder of what she'd already read and where she'd left off, repeating until the manuscript was done. That way, she could catch problems before I got too deeply into the story and things could be unraveled without tearing apart the entire manuscript. The read/feedback/edit looping process helped me learn how to catch mistakes before they derailed the story. As my self-editing skills improved, I learned to write faster and cleaner, and I was able to get more projects completed with less stress for me and for my editor.

190. Revising

Revising is part and parcel of being a novelist because it is the rare idea that comes out of your mind/fingers fully formed and ready to be presented to the world. Since you are telling a story from the prejudices of your own experiences, vocabulary, and time constraints, you might not realize your story could be confusing or misinterpreted by readers. That's why it's always a good idea to get feedback from a "considerate critiquer," meaning someone who understands the craft of storytelling and has your best interests in mind.

But it's not enough to collect feedback—you have to act on it to improve your story. Some writers hate to revise because they feel as if they're backtracking and tearing down something that took a lot of time to build. But working writers tend to appreciate the revision process because we see it as an opportunity to make our product as good as it can possibly be. It also helps to hone our skills so the next book is better.

191. How to handle criticism

One of the hardest lessons for a beginning (or advanced!) writer to learn is how and when to accept feedback. First, when it comes to soliciting feedback, be careful where you go. If you enter every writing contest indiscriminately without any thought to the relevance of the contest to your story, then don't be surprised if your feedback is all over the place. And I can't tell you how many times I've heard a writer complain that she asked someone to read her story and then after the person was generous enough to do it, the writer was angry the feedback wasn't to their liking. If you don't respect the person's opinion, then don't waste their time!

If the feedback you receive from another writer, a contest judge, an editor, or an agent isn't what you'd hoped, put the letter/notes away until you can regain some objectivity. Then read it again when emotions aren't running so high. Maybe even share it with a critique partner and see if they concur on some points. It's true some feedback is simply off base, but for the most part, if you simply let the advice soak in, you'll probably find a kernel of truth in there somewhere. Look at it this way: *Something* made the person reading your work react the way they did. You can either tell yourself they were mean/jealous/insane, or you can examine your work more closely for clues to what triggered the comments you found so objectionable.

192. Destructive criticism

You're a reasonable person, so you know, of course, not all the feedback you're going to get will be meaningful or relevant. And yes, some of it might even be nasty or cruel. But something about the story, scene, etc., triggered a negative reaction in the person who gave you feedback, so it behooves you to take a second look. No matter what, you have to suck it up, because it won't be the last time you'll hear something unflattering about your work.

Here's the thing: When you create something out of nothing and put it out in the world for other people to read, they're going to react to it. And that's okay...in fact, you *want* readers to react to it. Sure, it would be great if everyone loved it, and a lot of books are sold that way. But just as many books are sold because they polarized readers ("Loved the ending!" "Hated the ending!") Take a look at the reviews of some best-selling books and see what I mean. If readers are angry at you for doing something to a character, that means they're invested in your character, and that's a very good thing. Your relationship with readers is a two-way street. You give them something... they give you something back—that's how it works.

But if a critique partner regularly gives you feedback that's mean-spirited, you need to remove yourself from the situation. There are times when writers have to protect themselves. That doesn't mean you stick your head in the sand when people say something you don't want to hear, but you don't have to give haters more power than they deserve.

193. Interpreting feedback: "Amazing! Wonderful! Best story I've ever read!"

First, thank your mother like a good son or daughter. Then find someone more objective to read your manuscript. And when you do, don't badger them: "Did you read it yet? When are you going to? Did you like it? What part did you like best?"

Remember, you want the good news *and* the bad news. If it's the first time someone has critiqued for you, you might ask them to be alert for certain things, or give them a list of questions to respond to (keeping your weaknesses in mind): "Did you like the main character? What was your favorite part of the story? What was your least favorite part of the story?"

194. Interpreting feedback: "I don't like your character."

If someone says they don't like your main character, it isn't necessarily bad—if your main character is an anti-hero or anti-heroine, for example. Maybe they didn't like the character, but was fascinated by them. Or perhaps they thought the character was noble. But generally, this feedback means they wouldn't want to be in the same room with the person, so you would probably benefit from digging a little deeper—was there anything about the character they did like? Was there a tipping point for them regarding the character's behavior? It's possible you simply haven't made it clear *why* a character is behaving badly. Or you could be inadvertently making your character unlikable by making him/her too perfect—too beautiful, too talented, too rich, too lucky. Perfection triggers detachment.

195. Interpreting feedback: "I wasn't engaged."

Yawn. Not being engaged means the reader wasn't drawn into the story, they just skimmed over the surface. Check your pages for sensory detail, make sure you're showing versus telling, and analyze your point of view. Also, is the character someone the average reader can relate to, or aspire to be? Do you have enough at stake to compel the reader to keep turning the pages? Remember, you have to bring the reader into the character's world to convince the reader to take the journey with the character.

196. Interpreting feedback: "I couldn't follow the story."

If your reader got lost in your story (and not in a good way), you need to re-evaluate your scene logistics: Do you orient the reader at the beginning of every scene? Do you make it clear when people enter and exit the room? Do you use dialogue tags when appropriate to show who's speaking, especially when more than one person is talking? Do you have too many characters? Do you allude to characters traveling from point A to point B, or do they simply appear with no sense of time lapsing? And does your timeline make sense?

197. Interpreting feedback: "I'm confused as to what kind of book this is."

A comment from a reader that they're confused about the type of story means either the reader isn't familiar with the genre you're writing in, or you haven't made it clear your story is a mystery, a romance, a coming-of-age novel, etc. From the first sentence, you should be cueing the reader what to expect as far as story and tone. Keep in mind an unpublished novel doesn't have the benefit of back cover copy and a cover to indicate to the reader what kind of book lies within—it's all on you.

198. Interpreting feedback: "I don't have anything bad to say."

Yikes. When someone says they don't have anything bad to say about your novel, the implication is they also don't have anything *good* to say. There's nothing objectionable about the story…and nothing memorable. Your story is just lying there on the page, and nothing unexpected happened. To wake up your story, you need to fold in a surprise or two, a plot twist here and there, and maybe a new character to shake things up a little.

199. Interpreting feedback: "Your story feels episodic."

When someone says a manuscript is episodic, they mean it's choppy and there isn't a sense of transition between scenes or a progression of the story. The culprit might lie within your chapters—maybe they're too finite, too self-contained.

Let's say you're writing a mystery and in the beginning of every chapter your main character identifies a new suspect, but by the end of the chapter, has eliminated that suspect. And the same thing happens in the next chapter...and the next. That kind of structure will seem episodic (as in, similar to an episode of a TV show). You should strive to interweave everything so by the end of a chapter, some things from previous chapters are resolved, and new problems are introduced. By overlapping the introduction of new elements and tying up loose ends from earlier parts of your book, your story will seem less episodic.

200. Interpreting feedback: "Your story doesn't feel real."

When someone remarks your story doesn't feel real, you might be tempted to respond, "Of course it isn't real—this is fiction!" But even a story featuring paranormal elements should feel as if it *could* happen. Ground the reader in scenes with authentic and specific detail. Mix over-the-top elements with familiar elements. Intersperse dialogue with body language and movement. And make sure your dialogue rings true, that it isn't too stiff or too wordy.

201. Interpreting feedback: "I'm not sure where this story is going."

A story should be rolling toward some climactic event. If a reader isn't sure where the story is going, you haven't made it clear what your characters' goals are, and what obstacles they will face to get there. Or perhaps you haven't made it clear which character is the main character, i.e., who the reader should be rooting for. If your story direction is vague, review your story setup/pitch—make sure you can communicate the crux of your story in one or two sentences.

202. Interpreting feedback: "The title is *great.*"

If the only feedback you receive is your title is great, that's akin to not having anything good or bad to say about your story. In short—the reader doesn't think the story is living up to the promise of the title. Kudos on your great title—now make sure you're delivering more in your story than your reader expects. Amp up the conflict, the stakes, and the emotion! Make your reader care.

203. Imagination drill!

Readers love to see characters squirm! Your main character has their back against a wall and tells a whopper of a lie they'll have to make good on. Can you come up with 10 lies that would spin a fun story? I'll get the list started:

1. A teenage girl tells her friends she's bringing the hottest boy-band member on the planet to the senior prom.

2.

3.

4.

5.

6.

7.

8.

9.

10.

(For printable PDFs of all Imagination Drills, go to
www.stephaniebond.com.)

204. Changing for the sake of change

If you have one story idea, there are dozens...hundreds...thousands of ways to tell it. Maybe two or three of those ways are stellar...and a handful of those ways are just wrong, wrong, wrong. But the vast majority of the ways you can tell a story fall in the big group in between, which means one way to tell the story is just as good as another, they're each just as entertaining and compelling as the next. In other words, just because someone suggests you make a change to your story doesn't mean the change will make it better—or worse. Writers call this "changing for the sake of change" and there are lots of critique partners, contest judges, editors, line editors, copyeditors, and proofreaders out there who need to justify their job by suggesting a change. Or perhaps they just want to leave their mark on your story. When considering feedback, use critical judgment (and perhaps the opinion of someone else) to decide if the change would be only for the sake of change.

205. When is it time to say goodbye to an idea?

If you've been wallowing with several book ideas or partial manuscripts, now might be a good time for you to hit the "clear cache" button. Recently I was with a group of writers who were brainstorming ideas, and at least one writer admitted to clinging to an old idea perhaps a little longer than he should have.

It's true some ideas can simply become stale…but there's something very comfortable about holding on to a concept that's old and familiar. Sometimes it can be hard to let go because there might be a sense of failure associated with moving on. Writers tend to develop a "relationship" with their material, so letting go can feel as if you're turning your back on a good friend.

But at some point, you have to ask yourself if you're beating a dead horse. When you pitch the idea to your critique group and you're greeted an eye-roll and "Are you *still* working on that story?" you should stop and re-evaluate. Maybe the usefulness of the original idea was to help you learn things you can then apply to the *next* idea.

206. Recycling ideas

If you're of a certain age, you might remember the Paul Masson wine commercial where spokesman Orson Welles delivered the famous slogan, "We will sell no wine before its time." It can be like that with book ideas—some ideas are simply born before their time. Many years ago I had the inkling I wanted to write a mystery series about a body moving duo. But I couldn't make the characters work—a husband and wife? Girlfriend and boyfriend? Two sisters? Two brothers? Mother and daughter? I knew I wanted my main character to be a young contemporary woman, and I simply couldn't figure out why an attractive, hip woman would move bodies for the morgue. I didn't want someone who'd grown up in the business—she would be too knowledgeable, and that would eliminate the fish-out-of-water element. She wouldn't do it for money—there are too many other things she could do. Since I had other books under contract, I mentally shelved the idea while the pieces kept shuffling around in my mind.

Years later, I wrote *Party Crashers* that featured as a secondary character a young woman who worked at Neiman Marcus and who'd raised her younger brother who was constantly in trouble. And then it hit me—a young woman who felt parental toward her younger brother could get pulled into body moving if he got a job with the morgue and needed her help. Suddenly my *Body Movers* idea zoomed back to the forefront.

So even if you have to park a beloved idea for a while, if it's a robust concept, it will circle back around when its time comes.

207. When perfectionism becomes paralyzing

Perfectionism is the enemy of progress. Perfectionism in writing can manifest itself in several ways:

- You rewrite and rewrite your first few chapters before you can move on.
- You spend more time reading work you previously wrote than writing new pages.
- You're unable to let anyone critique your pages unless you believe the writing is perfect.
- Any negative feedback makes you defensive or puts you in a funk.
- You miss goals and deadlines because you're afraid to turn in pages you think will disappoint your editor/a contest judge, etc.

To fight perfectionism, you might need to make yourself accountable with a reward/penalty system to keep moving forward. Don't allow yourself to read previous work. And keep reminding yourself you can always go back and revise your story later after you write the first draft. Growing as a novelist means identifying weaknesses that keep you from meeting your goals, and facing them head-on.

GOING ON THE OFFENSE

When things start to get hard, you know you've ascended
to the next level. Time to redouble your effort!

208. The independent writer

It's important to seek out feedback on your writing from peers and from more advanced writers you can learn from. But there's a line between seeking feedback and relying on it. Don't become dependent on your critique partners to plot your stories, or to fix your characterization, or to correct your grammar. Your novel should not become a community project. It's important you become an independent writer who seeks out ways to improve your skillset, but at the same time, you grow in your own confidence and learn to trust your own judgment.

209. Invest in your writing career

I'm always surprised when writers balk at paying dues to writing organizations, costs to attend conferences, or fees to enter contests. Although the barrier to entry into the writing industry is low (you don't need a degree, pedigree, or experience), there are investments you can and should be willing to make to learn your craft, just as you would expect to make in learning any other vocation. Organization fees are typically low in return for access to workshops, newsletters, industry lists, contests, etc. And there are tools of the trade to make the process easier—robust equipment and updated word processing software. Don't go into debt to write your novel, but don't be cheap, and don't expect to get access to expert resources and instruction for free.

210. Build a reference library

I'm often asked if I still read writing how-to books and the answer is *yes!* I believe a writer never stops learning, and in fact, it's easy to become complacent, to fall into bad writing habits, over the course of several books. Reading how-to books is a good refresher for veteran writers, so I buy new how-to books that look interesting and reread keeper books on my how-to shelf (physical and digital). Since I'm working on a different project than when I first read the book, something in the material is bound to feel more relevant the second (or third) time around.

(I've included a section on reference books I recommend at the end of this book.)

211. Learn your word processing software

You can improve your productivity by learning the nuances of your word processing software—how to set up shortcuts for common keystrokes, how to create templates for your document formatting, how to use your online dictionary, thesaurus, and spelling tools to help you edit your document, and so much more. Word processing software has come so far in the last few years! Take a few minutes and go through free online tutorials to pick up techniques to help you spend less time making your manuscript look better and read better.

212. Improve your keyboarding skills

One often-overlooked way to become a more productive writer is to improve your typing/keyboarding skills. You might think you're doing okay with a hunt and peck method, but it could be getting in the way of your flow if your brain is waiting for your fingers to catch up. And if it's taking you a long time to get your thoughts down, you're probably nursing low-grade frustration every time you sit at the keyboard. How fast and how accurately can you type? Take an online typing speed test to gauge your skill level, and try to improve. You type more slowly when you compose versus simply re-typing/copying text, but you will benefit from becoming more familiar with the keyboard so you don't have to look at every keystroke—your fingers will just know where to go. (Wrists up, fingers light!)

213. Speech recognition software

Over the years I've experimented with speech recognition (SR) software, and the accuracy and ease of use has improved by leaps and bounds while the cost has gone down. The technology is finally to the point where I use it regularly. I used my SR software, in fact, to write sections of this book. Speech recognition software might be a good choice if you don't have great typing skills or have an injury or condition that prevents you from keyboarding comfortably. I was spurred to look into SR when a writing acquaintance suffered a wrist injury that put her way behind. It got me thinking about ways I can deviate from the traditional sitting-and-typing work position to extend my writing years into old age. With SR software, you can dictate wirelessly to your laptop while you're exercising or driving, for example, or dictate into a phone app and have the SR software "transcribe" your notes later. If you're accustomed to the trigger of your hands on the keyboard to jumpstart your thinking process, SR software will take some getting used to. But it's another tool to have in your kit.

214. Plotting software

There are various plotting software packages on the market to help you plan your book. Most of the packages use wizards of different levels of sophistication to walk you through questions and force you to think about things you might not have considered. Some packages also provide ways to document characters, settings, and details for series bibles including images, links to research, etc. I've used these packages with various levels of frustration and success. I suggest you use a trial version before investing in the full package, or ask for referrals from writing friends. If you're having trouble getting organized, plotting software can be useful to help you get your mind around your entire story.

215. Production widgets/apps

If you use applications to help manage your time/life, there are lots of tracking apps and widgets available to help you keep up with your production schedule. The apps can keep up with your wordcount, pagecount, and other inspirational stats. You can share apps with writing friends to monitor and challenge each other. Apps are especially helpful to keep you motivated when you're dividing your time between writing and other activities. Anything that prompts you to write is worth experimenting with.

216. Imagination drill!

A lonely man is celebrating Christmas alone. He hears a noise on the roof and suddenly something comes down the chimney. Can you think of 10 things it might be other than Santa Claus?

1.

2.

3.

4.

5.

6.

7.

8.

9.

10.

(For printable PDFs of all Imagination Drills, go to
www.stephaniebond.com.)

217. Attending conferences

I attribute the launch of my writing career to joining a national writing organization (Romance Writers of America), joining a local chapter, and attending various RWA conferences. At writing conferences you'll meet other writers at all levels, and have the opportunity to attend workshops on craft and the business of writing, plus network with industry professionals. You might also have the chance to meet with an editor to pitch your story during a short appointment.

For me, conferences are part business, part social occasion because I always learn something new and I get to reconnect with writing friends I rarely see. Plus it gives me a chance to gauge the "mood" of the industry—is everyone generally upbeat, or pessimistic? That's the kind of thing you can't always tell when communicating online or reading book news.

There are lots of writing conferences out there, for writers at every level and for every interest. Do your research to find the conference that's best for you and your budget.

218. Writing retreats

A writing retreat is typically different than a writing conference in setting, schedule, and goals. A retreat might have instruction built into the schedule, but the general sense is the setting is more casual, with the opportunity to quietly work on a project versus attending workshops in a classroom setting. Many retreats are held in vacation spots like the beach or the mountains to add an extra dimension of inspiration to your work-time. I've used writing retreats to undertake a writing marathon to finish a project, or to kickstart a new one. The change of scenery alone is sometimes enough to get those creative juices flowing, but it's also nice to be away from a desk stacked with paperwork, day to day chores, and people in our homes we have to schedule around.

I have a writing friend who, when facing the prospect of a writing marathon in order to meet a deadline, checks herself into a hotel for a few days. She takes with her a cooler full of snacks and drinks, and settles in for the duration. She says being away from her home and home office allows her to better focus, plus she has maid service and a restaurant at her disposal. Being away from daily distractions allows her to immerse herself in the manuscript and maintain erratic hours without impacting anyone else. In the long run, it's better for her, her business, and her family.

219. Creative solitude

Over my writing career, I've shared my space with other people and I've lived alone...and I have to say I kind of love living alone. I revel in my creative solitude. Every person's mind expands when there's silence, but in the absence of distractions, a writer's mind expands a hundredfold. This phenomenon explains why we're introverts; we don't need to be entertained because we can entertain ourselves! Think-time is necessary to our process, but to others, it can seem selfish and exclusionary. Non-creatives see us staring off into space and assume we're daydreaming, while inside our brains are sprinting, planning, devising. It's how we're wired.

You might have already recognized your need for creative solitude, but if not, know that scheduling quiet time for yourself will be an absolute must for your mental well-being—and for your success as a novelist.

220. How to find a writing conference/retreat

At any given time, a writing conference is happening somewhere in the world. The Internet makes it easy to research conferences, and postings/websites can be very telling regarding the quality of the coordination—a conference thrown together haphazardly or at the last minute might not provide the best experience. Also, will the conference coordinators help you find lodging and transportation, or are you on your own?

Carefully research the conference content before you sign up—does it cater mostly to readers, to writers, or to industry professionals? Is the atmosphere more casual or more business-like? Is the location a destination you can easily access or will travel time factor into your decision? Also, regarding location, note that (excluding cruises) the more resort-like the location, the fewer opportunities you'll have to network because attendees will be scattered to the beach, spa, sightseeing, etc. If you can find someone who attended the conference the previous year(s), ask what things they most liked/disliked about the conference. Do the workshops look interesting and will you have the opportunity to buy tapes of the workshops you liked or missed? If you decide to attend the conference, register as early as possible to qualify for early-bird discounts; some conferences offer incentives to register early, such as special drawings or exclusive opportunities to network.

221. Before a conference

Getting the most out of a writing conference requires a little pre-planning. Go armed with your own goals—do you want to pitch an idea to an editor? Learn how to fix a problem with your story? Meet other writers in your area? Have the opportunity to speak to a published author you admire? Do some fact-finding ahead of time—know who's attending and something about them so if you encounter them during the conference, you can have a meaningful conversation.

Be aware it's easy to feel overwhelmed at your first writing conference. Attending a conference when you've just begun writing is like tuning into a TV series that's well underway. At first, you'll be confused, but the more you watch (and learn), things will begin to fall into place; you'll soon be able to identify names and faces in the industry, while picking up tips to improve your writing skills.

222. After a conference

During my writing career, I've met lots of professional conference attendees. They sign up for every conference within travel distance. Once there, they attend every workshop they can and buy tapes of the ones they missed. They take notes and ask good questions and buy how-to books written by the instructors. They get an A+ for being the best little writing student ever.

But when they return home, they never get around to putting what they learned into action. It seems obvious, but it's worth mentioning—it's not enough to simply sit in on a workshop, listen to a podcast, or read a how-to book; you have to apply what you've learned to your work-in-progress or your career…else why bother?

223. How-to overload

There's a delicate balance between learning enough about the industry to be well-informed, and learning so much you begin to shut down creatively. Some writers thrive on attending conferences—they rejuvenate me, although admittedly I typically attend only 1-2 per year. But I recall a multi-published writer telling me attending big conferences made her feel like a very small fish in a very large pond; it overwhelmed her to the point that when she returned home, she was paralyzed in her writing and in her thinking. Other writers react the same way to reading about first-sales or other book deals—they're so intimidated or swayed by what other writers are selling, it affects their work. Similarly, many writers report compulsively checking their online sales rankings or royalties reports. Still other writers allow reviews to guide their outlook.

The point is, there's a ton of information out there, and it's important to know information in and of itself doesn't mean a lot if you don't have a framework in which to judge its usefulness. The difference between a book on Amazon being ranked 50,000 and 500,000 might be only a handful of books sold combined with something as irrelevant as the first letter of your title. Don't waste your time on things that ultimately can't help and in fact, will only confuse. Consider the motivation/angle of the person/organization providing the information you're reading. Writer email loops are notorious for being purveyors of anecdotal info. And what applies to someone else and their books won't necessarily apply to you and yours. If an experience or piece of information lessens your desire to write, can it, like my writing friend who ditched conferences.

Over time you'll learn which resources are the most helpful to you and you'll filter out those useful bits. I'm constantly tweaking my resources—looking for new ones and discarding the ones no longer applicable to my career. Striking a balance between enough information and too much information is just one more decision you'll have to make as a writer.

224. Visualization

Professional athletes and self-help gurus evangelize visualization techniques to increase the probability of an action/result occurring. One way I use visualization to help me improve a manuscript is to imagine the relationship I have with my characters, who are real to me, and the obligation I have to write a good story for them. I imagine the main character of my *Body Movers* mystery series, Carlotta Wren, sitting in the extra chair in my office, legs crossed, filing her nails. She says to me, "Okay, what next, Bond? Don't make me boring."

Or if I'm stuck on a manuscript—let's say I'm having trouble with the sagging middle. I'll skip ahead and write the cover letter to my editor: "I'm especially proud of the way I was able to keep the pacing tight in the middle of the story." And then I elaborate on what I did to keep it "tight." In other words, I pretend I've already worked out the problem. And in almost every case, in the midst of the pretending, I get an idea of how to do just that.

Another time in my career, I was hoping to sell a new series idea and I had in mind the amount of advance I wanted for it. So I created a mock-up check made out to me in that amount and posted it on my computer. It motivated me when I wrote the pitch for the series and later, when my agent and I negotiated the deal. The outcome? I was offered a tad more than the check I'd written to myself and to this day, I don't think it would've happened if I hadn't first visualized it.

225. What motivates you?

What motivates you? Accomplishment? Love? Money? Revenge? I'm a writer because I love to create stories, but I admit when I'm in a slump, I pull out a particular rejection letter I received early in my career that was so thoroughly dismissive, in hindsight I'm surprised I didn't quit. Lots of successful writers tell similar tales during banquet speeches—how a cruel critique or bruising rejection letter meant to make them question their aspirations, instead made them redouble their efforts.

As it turns out, when someone tells me I can't/shouldn't do something, I see it as a challenge…and I'm not about to give that person the satisfaction of seeing me quit.

I'm also motivated by seeing a row of my completed books on a shelf. And seeing the planned cover art of a manuscript I'm trying to finish always helps me get to the end. And that pesky mortgage hanging over my head is always a good motivator!

No matter what you do in life, it's important to surround yourself with things that motivate you to dig deeper, reach higher, go farther.

226. Two types of writers—which type of you?

After giving countless writing workshops, I've determined there are basically two types of writers: ones who are serious about finishing their novel, and ones who simply like the idea of calling themselves writers. How can I tell the difference?

- Writers who aren't serious talk about their story nonstop.
- Writers who are serious ask questions.

- Writers who aren't serious seek feedback, but don't revise.
- Writers who are serious seek feedback and make considerate revisions.

- Writers who aren't serious attend writing meetings to socialize.
- Writers who are serious attend writing meetings to learn.

- Writers who aren't serious make excuses.
- Writers who are serious join a critique group.

- Writers who aren't serious don't read.
- Writers who are serious read in their genre and read widely.

- Writers who aren't serious think their book can't be defined.
- Writers who are serious educate themselves about the market.

- Writers who aren't serious believe editing is someone else's job.
- Writers who are serious submit their best effort.

- Writers who aren't serious refuse to let go of a story that's stale.
- Writers who are serious develop fresh, new ideas.

- Writers who aren't serious grouse about the cost of dues and conferences.
- Writers who are serious invest in their career.

- Writers who aren't serious think they don't have to follow rules.
- Writers who are serious learn submission protocol.

- Writers who aren't serious talk about writing.
- Writers who are serious *write*.

Which type of writer are you?

227. Good stress, bad stress

I shake my head when I see articles and news segments about living a stress-free life. If you're over the age of twelve, I'm not sure it's possible to live a stress-free life—or desirable.

The media and medical experts have painted stress as negative, something that makes your blood pressure rise, your waistline expand, and generally decreases the quality of your life. And it's true high-stress over long-term situations can have a negative impact on your physical and mental well-being.

But not all stress is bad. There's such a thing as *good* stress. Good stress pushes you to put in one more hour of preparation before a big test or interview. Good stress helps you to kick it up a notch the last five minutes of your workout or when the finish line is in sight. Good stress gives you the inspiration to come up with an idea for something you wouldn't have thought of under normal circumstances. It's the blend of nervous excitement and fear that spikes adrenaline to give you a little "oomph" to get the job done.

Good stress raises your performance level.

Good stress is our friend. The trick is channeling it. When you feel a tickle of dread in your stomach over the task ahead of you, embrace it. Recognize what it can do for you. And tackle the task head-on before that energizing *good* stress turns into paralyzing *bad* stress.

228. How do you handle pressure?

It's good to know how you handle writing under pressure before you put yourself in a position of having to do it. I know some writers who totally crumble under pressure, and other writers who seem to thrive under added stress. I confess I work well under pressure—and let me assure you, I'm not patting myself on the back. When a writer knows he/she works well under pressure, they might be tempted to procrastinate, then burn the midnight oil to meet a deadline. And since life tends to interfere (illness, family emergency, natural disaster, computer failure) at the most inconvenient moments, using pressure to motivate yourself isn't the best plan. Obviously there's a lot of room for a happy medium between curling into a fetal positon and having masochistic tendencies. Find your happy place.

229. Two of your biggest enemies

If you decide to become a writer, two of your biggest enemies aren't rejection and poverty; two of your biggest enemies are frustration and boredom. Which, if you think about it, applies to almost everything in life: school, relationships, and whatever you choose to do for a living—even your hobbies. Everyone is excited in the initial phases of an endeavor because it's new! It's shiny! It's fun!

And then things start to feel routine, maybe even a little mundane. Especially if you have a goal in mind and you don't seem to be making progress, or even, *gulp*, losing ground! Most people give up on creative goals like writing, acting, learning to play a musical instrument or speaking a new language because they reach a plateau and boredom sits in.

So how do you keep things interesting? Keep mixing things up, or maybe change the environment. For writers, that might mean writing something new, or changing the venue where you write. Or joining a new writers group, or changing critique groups, or subscribing to a daily podcast...or even changing the wallpaper on your computer screen.

Your brain and your body need to be challenged constantly to remain alert and to continue to develop. When you feel frustration and boredom begin to set it, don't walk away—change things up!

230. Your WORST enemy

I mentioned frustration and boredom will be two of your biggest enemies on the journey of writing your novel, and now I want to alert you to the biggest enemy you will encounter along the way: *You.*

Over the years, I've listened to countless writers complain about their editor, agent, critique group, spouse, fellow writers, on and on with the list of people who seem to be working against them, yet after a while it becomes clear *they* are the single biggest obstacle to their own success. They procrastinate, they're stubborn, they reject feedback, or become manic. Some of that comes from working in a vacuum that allows bad habits to develop…which leads to missed deadlines and stress…which leads to a short fuse.

While I've witnessed legitimate situations where a writer had to sidestep an irrational adversary, the vast majority of the time, a writer's nemesis is in the mirror.

231. Staying accountable

Making a plan, setting goals, creating a to-do list—all of those organizational tasks are worthwhile and you should absolutely do them. But just as important as the planning is the follow-through. And in order to follow-through on your good intentions, you need to figure out a way to stay accountable to your plan for when things get boring or hard. If you're self-disciplined, then being accountable to yourself might be enough. If you respond better when someone else holds you accountable, then coordinate with a friend. Many writing groups sponsor "finish the book" contests if competition motivates you. Or if you're really brave, you could use social media to post goals and make yourself accountable to your followers.

232. A marathon writing day

I mentioned in a previous segment how my books are generally finished thirty minutes here, fifteen minutes there. But nothing catapults my page count like one long marathon writing day. If you find yourself with a snow day or can schedule ahead for an uninterrupted day, take advantage of it. A marathon writing day can get you past a plateau, the sagging middle, or barreling toward the finish line. For the most effective marathon writing day:

- Get a good night's sleep.
- Set an ambitious production goal for the day, and share it with someone.
- Have your synopsis/outline finished and at-hand.
- Know what scenes you're going to write before you sit down.
- Turn off the phone, email, text notifications, etc.
- Put a "Do not disturb" sign on your door. (I remove my electronic doorbell.)
- Find a music channel on the TV for background noise you don't have to tend to.
- Stock up on food and drink for quick meals and snack breaks.
- Use a timer to break down your writing time into 30-minute sprints.
- Keep pushing even if you get a little tired—it's only one day!

233. Imagination drill!

A young boy who's being bullied at school wishes for a super power—and gets one. Can you think of 10 embarrassing things he has to use/wear/say, etc. to engage his super power?

1.

2.

3.

4.

5.

6.

7.

8.

9.

10.

(For printable PDFs of all Imagination Drills, go to
www.stephaniebond.com.)

234. Taking stock

I suggest you don't constantly go back and read what you've written—that's a surefire way to stall out, and to fall in love with your words to the point that you can't revise if necessary. That said, it's not a bad idea to set a few mile-markers in your manuscript—perhaps one-third and two-thirds of the way in—to stop and read everything from the beginning to check your pacing and see if you have any plot holes. If you have a critique partner, they might be reading a chapter or two at a time, and some things (such as flow) can be overlooked if the story is being read episodically. If you have problems, it's best to catch them now so you can correct course versus expounding on those problems. The next ten segments discuss the top reasons manuscripts are rejected (by editors *and* by readers)—use them as a checklist when you take stock of your work-in-progress.

235. Top reasons novels are rejected: "Wrong length."

From a writer's perspective, a book is as long as it needs to be to tell the story. But from an editor's perspective, a manuscript has to fit within the general wordcount constraints already in place at the publishing house, to keep their offerings consistent within a range. Publishers are concerned about paper usage, how many books fit into standard shipping boxes, and how the books will be shelved and priced at the retail level. So an editor can't purchase a manuscript that's way too short or way too long without a lot of revising… which probably means she'll pass. Read the publishers' guidelines to get an idea of the range of wordcount they're looking for, and know there are business reasons for adhering to those lengths.

236. Top reasons novels are rejected:

"Manuscript is too writerly."

Writers tend to react to the pressure of producing something of quality by using big words and obscure phrases or purple prose. Literary novelists can get away with writing that's more introspective and lyrical. But commercial fiction novelists should use language that's more straightforward. Regardless of the type of novel you write, flowery language is a telltale sign of a beginning writer, as are clichéd genre elements that seem gratuitous or hackneyed. When a manuscript is rejected for being "too writerly," it means the writer jammed their manuscript full of stock characters and phraseology and situations they *thought* they were expected to write.

237. Top reasons novels are rejected: "Opening isn't compelling."

You get one page, maybe two, to grab the editor's attention. If that seems unfair, consider the fact the editor is squeezing in the job of reading manuscripts for possible acquisition in between her main duties of acquiring, editing, and managing manuscripts for the stable of authors she already has. Finding and buying a new author is exciting, but it's kind of a pain, too. It means the editor might have to work with a new agent, or with an unagented author who needs their hand held when it comes to processing contracts. And for all she knows, it took you ten years to write the manuscript, and she's going to need a manuscript from you every year. All these things are going through her head when she's reading your manuscript, so it has to be more than good to be worth her trouble—it has to be great. And since she has twenty-five more manuscripts to sample on her train ride home, if your book doesn't grab her from the first sentence, it will likely get a pass. Don't hold back—give her the good stuff right up front.

238. Top reasons novels are rejected:

"No market for this type of book."

Every editor laments getting a well-written submission that doesn't fit any of their "lines." Make sure you read all publishers' guidelines to see what type of books are being bought—you will likely see the same genres and phrases used over and over. (Many publishers' guidelines will also state what they're *not* looking for.) If your manuscript doesn't fit the description of what publishers are seeking, is there a way you can move it closer toward a sellable book? Closer to the type of story a reader will recognize and will take a gamble on?

239. Top reasons novels are rejected: "Writer doesn't understand rules of genre."

When you attempt to write a type of book that already has a big readership (like romance), you're increasing your odds of success when you present your book to the market. But when you tell an editor or a reader what genre your book is, you had better know what the rules of the genre are and demonstrate you understand those parameters. Readers of genre fiction will expect certain types of characters, situations, language, certain levels of sex and violence, and resolution. Resist the temptation to go rogue and give the editor something wildly different to set your manuscript apart—especially with your first novel. An editor will want to see that you know the rules before she'll let you break them.

240. Top reasons novels are rejected: "Main character isn't heroic/redeemable."

The main character has to do something that is not only self-less, but is counter to their purposes, for the greater good. If your main character breaks a law or moral code, they have to have a good reason. Consider the following situations and come up with at least one good reason a reader would excuse the bad behavior from a main character:

- Saying something unkind
- Breaking into a house
- Shoplifting
- Lying to a spouse
- Striking an elderly person
- Taking someone's life

Most readers who choose novels are looking for an escape from their problems, and prefer to read about characters who are better/wiser/braver/more heroic than the people they come in contact with every day. Does your main character live up to their expectations?

241. Top reasons novels are rejected:

"Main character acts out of character."

Stating your character acts "out of character" is a way of saying the character is all over the board—tender one moment, angry the next, strong and silent, then super chatty. Your character's personality type should be set from the beginning of the story. And while you should be putting them in situations where they can/are forced to grow emotionally, you shouldn't have them suddenly act out of character for no reason. If a character is afraid of commitment, for example, they need a very good reason to make that leap. Or there should be some half-steps in between, and maybe a setback or two. Keep in mind a character should act consistently in all parts of their life—in their professional life and personal life, in the boardroom and in the bedroom, until they have a revelation that moves them forward emotionally. Your main character is the compass of your story—if they're not a steady needle, your story will be all over the map.

242. Top reasons novels are rejected:
"Story too predictable."

On the other end of the spectrum of "writer doesn't understand rules of genre" is "story too predictable," meaning the editor has seen the story before. An earlier segment mentioned the challenges of writing within the confines of a genre's formula, yet making it fresh. Your story should have a few scenes that surprise, shock, or yank the story in an unexpected direction. Remember the editor is a reader, too—a jaded one, because she's read a lot of great manuscripts, and a lot of not-so-great manuscripts. Delight her with something she hasn't seen before yet she knows will please her/your audience.

243. Top reasons novels are rejected:

"Plot movements too convenient."

Readers like conflict and obstacles, and characters who have to work hard to overcome adversity. To that end, you should derail your character—let them be wrong sometimes, or be misled or betrayed. Or maybe they get to the right place, but a few minutes late. In general, your book shouldn't read as if everyone and Mother Nature is making things easy for your main character. The villain should have the upper hand for a while. Even characters who mean well might inadvertently cause problems. Just make sure things don't fall into place for your main character—he/she has to be proactive about finding solutions. So if they're on the run for their life and they come up on a ravine that's too deep to cross, instead of providing a downed tree that spans the opening, force your hero/heroine to chop down a tree...with a dull axe... that they have to steal. Your character should be willing to do anything to achieve their goal—make him/her work for it.

244. Top reasons novels are rejected:
"Resolution too easy."

In an earlier segment, I mentioned the Black Moment of the story, which is where the conflict reaches a climax. In a thriller, it's the moment where the main character's life is hanging in the balance as they are pitted against the villain. In a romance novel, it's where the hero and heroine believe their relationship has no chance. Remember, this isn't the "brown moment," or the "gray moment"—it's the *black* moment. For a moment, *all hope is lost*. And then...the character summons an inner strength he/she didn't know they had and does something to overcome the villain or the internal conflict that's standing in the way of happiness.

But the resolution can't be too easy. And it should be a grand gesture. The resolution is the capstone of everything you and your character have been working for, so milk it.

245. Imagination drill!

A woman finds a $100 bill on the sidewalk and decides to pocket it. What are 10 things she can do with the $100 that lead to surprising consequences? I'll do the first one and a half:

1. She uses the money to pay a late bill, but it turns out the money is counterfeit.

2. She drops it into a Salvation Army donation bucket, but

3.

4.

5.

6.

7.

8.

9.

10.

(For printable PDFs of all Imagination Drills, go to
www.stephaniebond.com.)

246. Using aids to enhance creativity

The image of creative types boozing it up or being stoned is played up in movies and books, so I can see why someone would think it would be a creativity booster. But in my opinion, with the exception of caffeine, using a chemical aid to amp up creativity is a total myth. While my critique group and I have been known to brainstorm some good titles while drinking a glass of wine, if I need to actually work—i.e., get real pages done—I steer clear of alcohol because it puts me to sleep. And any writer, artist, musician, etc., who relies on alcohol or drugs to help them be more creative is traveling down a self-destructive road. Speaking for myself, I need every single one of my brain cells. Writing is hard enough—don't make the journey more arduous by adding chemical dependency to the mix. (For a natural stimulant I like that's readily available in many forms, see the next segment.)

247. The power of peppermint

When you need to write, but you find your focus wandering or your body growing tired, try peppermint to pep yourself up and get your creativity hopping again. Peppermint gum is a great pick-me-up. And when I need some extra staying power, I soak a cotton ball with peppermint oil and put it in a small cloth pouch around my neck. Peppermint candy can also put the spring back in your brain, and you get the added boost of sugar. Peppermint scented candles, incense, and hand lotion can also give you added energy. Even swishing with peppermint mouthwash will wake you up and give you more stamina.

248. Tactile brainstorming

Authorities in learning processes will tell you not all children perform well in a classroom setting—sitting in a hard chair, in a row, staring straight ahead at the blackboard—because the environment is not optimal for the way some children naturally learn. Sometimes visual and audio cues aren't enough to get the brain engaged, which is why I encourage you to add sensory triggers to your work setting, like scented candles and chewing gum. If you're a tactile learner, meaning doing something hands-on is the optimal way for you to learn, you might consider doing something with your hands when you brainstorm. If merely setting your hands on the keyboard doesn't get the creative juices flowing, try tossing a ball up in the air or against a wall...or squeezing a tennis ball, or peeling an apple, or working Silly Putty. The tactile, repetitive activity might be the trick to get your imagination rolling.

249. Not writing

Just as writing can become a habit, not writing can also become a habit. In fact, sometimes the longer you stay away from your writing, the harder it can be to return. I'm not talking about external circumstances that prevent you from writing—I'm talking about the gnaw in your gut when you think about writing that makes you do something more fun, more immediate, and less frustrating than writing. The more you give in to that sensation, the more power it has over you. But *you* are in control—only you can establish the good habit of writing or the bad habit of not writing.

250. The curse of being many-sided

When I talk to writers, it doesn't take long before the conversation reveals they have lots of interests, perhaps dual college degrees, many career experiences, travel, hobbies, etc. And some of those interests might seem opposing in nature, such as a passion for technology and for art. What I've learned over the years is most fiction writers are considered a Jack-of-all-trades, which makes sense when you think about it—what better person to create their own little worlds?

But having varied interests can work against you when you try to finish your novel because everything will beckon to you—those unfinished craft or home renovation projects, the books you haven't finished reading, the gift you need to stop and make, the phone app you feel compelled to learn. The personality trait that drove you to writing—your boundless curiosity—can also pull you away from writing. I have to fight the urge to paint and sew because I've learned they drain my creative energy and negatively impact my writing time. If the progress on your novel has slowed, take care you're not spreading your creative resources too thin. You multi-talented person, you.

251. Confusing writing activities with writing

I know so many writers who are busy, yet never seem to get manuscripts written. They spend all their time planning a book, chatting with writer friends, attending conferences, buying productivity tools, or posting to social media. Just to clarify:

- Talking about writing isn't writing.
- Thinking about writing isn't writing.
- Learning about writing isn't writing.
- Buying writing tools, books, and equipment isn't writing.

Only writing is writing. Go write.

252. Perseverance and flexibility

On the surface, perseverance and flexibility seem to counter each other; instead, they go hand in hand. Perseverance doesn't mean you dig in your heels and keep doing the same thing until you succeed. If you receive advice that seems organic to you, fold it into your career plan, and keep moving forward. Perseverance means you simply find ways *not to quit*. Adjusting your future behavior based on lessons learned from past behavior is what humans do best. So, keep keeping on, but use your good common sense to make adjustments as you move forward. If you've been beating your head against a wall for several years trying to make something happen with your novel, then it's probably time for a change in tactics. To paraphrase Henry Ford: If you keep doing what you're doing, you keep getting what you've got.

253. Saboteurs

In the beginning, people are generally excited and supportive of your goal to write a novel—it's so cool! And brave! And cool!

Until it's a drag. Because you're not going out to lunch anymore. And you always have your nose stuck in your computer. And you talk about your characters as if they're real people. And you make everyone else feel as if what they do isn't as special as what you do. Hurry up and finish writing that book! Not because we want you to publish it—we don't care anymore. We want you to put aside what's important to you and do what's important to us!

Oh, you actually published your book? Phew, thank goodness! Glad you got that out of your system. Wait—you're going to write *another* book? You mean, you're going to do this again? Why? You don't really think you're going to make a living at this, do you? Your first book was okay, but....

And so it goes. Don't be surprised if at some point, supporters become saboteurs...passive-aggressive...resentful...even denigrating. It happens if the dynamics in a relationship shift—i.e., suddenly you're getting more attention or demanding more alone-time or you're acting suspiciously happy and fulfilled.

Acknowledge why the person's feelings have morphed—because they don't want things to change. And there might be a little jealousy at play because you're pursuing a dream (and they aren't?). Be magnanimous and approachable, persuasive and inclusive, but relationships are a two-way street—as your interests change and grow, the people who care about you should be willing to accept and support those interests.

254. Read something great

When I can't get in the mood to write, I go to my overloaded bookshelves and pull books at random, books I've been waiting for a chance to read, and dive in. I let the story carry me along and think, *Wow, that's really good. I'm so impressed with the way the writer developed this character…or surprised me with that plot twist…or made me stay up late to finish the story.* Reading a great book never fails to inspire me to get back to my own writing with renewed energy because I know at some point, the writer struggled with their story, had doubts about it ever being done, sweated and cried and bled over the keyboard… yet they kept at it and now they have a good book to show for their efforts. Reading something great inspires me to get back to my work-in-progress and put everything I have into it.

255. Read something terrible

On the flipside of reading something great to be inspired, I get equally inspired by reading something terrible! I've read my share of clunker books, many of them bestsellers. And although I might begrudge the time and money I invested in the book, reading a not-so-great book is a useful exercise because I can spot the clunky dialogue, the plot holes, the melodrama, the rushed ending. It's also a reminder to me if the story is good enough, readers will overlook less than remarkable writing. I pulled one of my old Nancy Drew books from the shelf recently to scan a few pages and was appalled at the bad writing and the proliferation of exclamation points!!! Yet as a young reader, I didn't notice any of those things; I was simply pulled along by the characters and the story. And before you run down a bestseller that, to your eye and sensibility, has problems, remember the author did at least two things right—he/she finished writing their novel, and they put it out into the universe. Will you?

256. Don't write!

I'm often lovingly crushed with visitors, so I can attest there's something about not being allowed to write that makes you think of writing! It's like someone telling you not to think about a pink elephant—as soon as the words leave their mouth, you can't think about anything *but* a pink elephant. When something keeps you from writing, inexplicably your mind turns to what you'd be writing if only you could. A writer friend told me the way she jumpstarted her writing when she was going through a slump was by forbidding herself to write for an entire week. By the time the week was over, she was panting to get back to the computer. "No Writing Week" might be an interesting exercise to try with your critique group.

257. Directed brainstorming

Before I go for a run or do any kind of exercise, if I'm working on a manuscript, I practice what I call "directed brainstorming." All that means is I look at my synopsis/chapter outline to see what's coming up next, and I think about those scenes, try to play them out in my head, cinema-style. I play out the same scene/situation over and over and almost without fail I'll come up with extra details or small twists I hadn't thought of before. Directed brainstorming makes the scene much easier to write when I get to it. And as a bonus, it makes my workout seem to go by faster. (I sometimes practice directed brainstorming before I go to sleep, too, to let my subconscious work on my story problems. If you try it, keep a pen and paper next to your bed.)

258. Ask leading questions

Another way of getting unstuck is to type leading questions to yourself, such as: *What would be a good way to start this chapter? What can my character do or say right now that would be most unexpected? What can I bring forward from a previous chapter to build on? How can I make the situation more dire?*

I keep typing questions and answers until something good comes to me. Writers respond well when presented with questions—we feel compelled to answer them, even if we're posing the questions to ourselves. Use that compulsion to move your story past a plateau.

259. Talk it out—with yourself

Similar to asking leading questions, talking out my scenes (dictating them and typing as I talk) always jumpstarts my creativity. Just hearing my voice seems to stimulate another part of my brain—it keeps me moving forward, and is especially helpful in writing dialogue scenes. There's something about hearing words spoken that brings more words and more sentences to mind, as if you're having a conversation. "Talk" to yourself while you're writing and before you know it, your story will be flowing and the paragraphs will start piling up.

260. Someone quit today

In the beginning of this book, I mentioned there were three secrets to writing a novel, and the third one is "Find ways not to stop until you get to The End." And I meant it.

A few years ago, a writing acquaintance told me she was feeling defeated trying to write and sell her first book, and she felt like quitting. She asked if I had any advice. I told her to envision a room full of aspiring writers. Statistics tell us only a handful of them will finish their novel and fewer still will be published. Every few days, some of the writers will quit for various and sundry reasons, and as time goes on, they will drop away faster and faster. I said, "Someone quit today—is that you? If it's you, you'll increase the odds that someone else in that room is going to make it." She visibly pulled herself up and said, "I'm not quitting."

About a year later I received a nice note from her saying our conversation had stuck with her and had spurred her to get serious about her writing career. She had just accepted a deal with a top publisher and was so glad she hadn't quit. (It was sweet of her to give me some credit, but she did all the work.)

Someone quit today. They shoved their unfinished novel back under the bed or ejected a CD and tucked it away in a drawer, or deleted the computer files altogether. They will never realize their dream of being a novelist. But not you—you're barreling ahead!

261. Imagination drill!

A bored teenager visiting his grandfather snoops in the attic and finds a locked trunk. What he finds inside turns his world upside down. Can you think of 10 different scenarios?

1.

2.

3.

4.

5.

6.

7.

8.

9.

10.

(For printable PDFs of all Imagination Drills, go to
www.stephaniebond.com.)

262. Force a conversation
between your characters

If you're stalled on what scene to write next, consider forcing a conversation between two characters. For instance, have a secondary character pose a provocative question to a main character. (The conversation could be over the phone or in-person or text—people respond differently if they're standing in front of someone versus talking on the phone or in the short form of texting.) In my experience, freeform dialogue writing always leads to interesting places. Even if I don't keep the entire scene, there's bound to be a kernel of something good in there.

263. Your characters deserve closure

There was a commercial on TV a while back that featured a kid jumping off a diving board and being "frozen" in midair because the person who took a picture of him left it in their camera/phone (didn't print it). The kid chastised the picture-taker for leaving him hanging there all that time. One way I force myself to keep going with a story is to visualize my characters "frozen" in the spot where I left them. Until I finish the story, I'm leaving my characters "hanging" in midair, and that's not fair—they deserve closure.

264. When you lose focus (literally)

Your first novel will be the hardest you will write because every page, scene, and plot turn will seem like you're hacking a path through a jungle using a dull hatchet. You will be tired, and at some point, your focus will wander. Chances are good your focus will blur because you're not sure where to go next with the story. But if you find yourself easily distracted and getting up from your computer a lot, there could be a physiological explanation: Consider having your eyesight checked. If you're not accustomed to sitting in front of the computer for extended bouts of writing, your eyes might be strained. Or if you have glasses/contact lenses, it might be time for a new prescription. At the very least, you should keep eye drops at your desk and set reminders to give your peepers a break.

265. Write SOMEthing

Even if you work from an outline, sometimes a scene just won't come. If you're completely stuck and frustrated (or out of practice), skip ahead and write a scene you know you're going to need eventually, such as a great love scene, the black moment, or even the ending. Remember, writing begets writing. Write *some*thing.

266. Not in the mood

Occasionally (and not nearly often enough), we all have one of those days when we leap out of bed and race to our laptop to write something before it disappears into the ether, when things are clicking along and we're firing on all cylinders. We're in a zone! And conversely, we all have those days when we're...not. That's okay. Some days you will simply feel and be more creative than other days. The trick is to push yourself on the good days, and to have workarounds for the days you're not in the mood. The most successful novelists have the most workarounds.

267. Observation skills

Writers have lots of skills (inherent and learned) other people don't have, including keen observation skills. Where one person might see a lady walking down the street, a writer would notice her shoes are different colors, or that she's wearing a wig. Writers can also assess a person or a scene and get a sense of mood—is something off? Is the person behaving strangely? Is something about to happen? I'm not sure why we seem to be expert people-watchers... perhaps it has something to do with most of us being introverts at heart— most of us would rather watch a performance than do the performing. If you're stuck in your novel, or need a jumping off place for a scene, a subplot, or a turning point, use your observation skills to pluck an idea from your surroundings. The next ten segments are observation exercises to strengthen your imagination muscles.

268. Observation exercise: Outside a window

For this exercise, go to the nearest window and focus on the first object that catches your eye—a fly? A dying geranium? A mailbox? Figure out a way to incorporate the object into your story. I'll use all three:

Let's say I'm writing a mystery. I might have a single fly lead the detective to a dead body. Or a dying geranium next to three healthy ones might be a tip-off that poison was used and the killer ditched the rest of it on the plant as he fled. Or a mailbox in front of an abandoned home might be the perfect place for scheming criminals to exchange notes.

Try it!

269. Observation exercise: Make up a story about a stranger

For this observation exercise, you'll have to interact with/be around other people. Pick a stranger who's in a good position for you to observe (don't stare and make them uneasy), and make up a story about them. I do this when I eat alone:

The quiet guy at the table with his raucous buddies? He's worried about something going on at home, but can't bring himself to leave the party. Maybe his teenage son is into drugs...or he thinks his wife is cheating on him. Or maybe he's being bullied by his neighbor.

The pretty girl at the bar who looks as if she could cry any second? Her boss asked her to do something illegal and she doesn't know what to do. Or her sister has been missing for three days. Or she just heard her ex is getting married.

The older guy working behind the bar? He lost his retirement in an investment scam and had to get a second job. Or his dream is to own a beach bar, so he's learning the ropes. Or he's on the run from a crime he committed a decade ago, working for cash under the table to stay off the grid.

When you invent backgrounds and stories for strangers, you might be surprised how much compassion and insight it gives you for people in general, and how much it will inform your writing.

270. Observation exercise: Observe a room in your home

This observation exercise is to make you more aware of things in your everyday surroundings you've become immune to. Walk into a room in your home and analyze it from a stranger's point of view. What would a neighbor surmise about you? A criminal? A coworker? Would they be surprised? Shocked? Amused? Are there things in the room that aren't yours but look as if they might be? (The misdelivered X-rated toy catalog you haven't gotten around to tossing?) Does the room smell like mothballs? Wet dog? Loneliness? Look in the corners and under things. Do you find dust bunnies? Mislaid papers? A treasure you hid and forgot about?

Don't get so waylaid that you forget about the pages you need to write that day! But everything you learn about yourself is something you can attribute to one of your characters.

271. Observation exercise: Take a walk

For this exercise, you're going to get some! Take a walk around the block, to the park, or even to your backyard, and focus intently on sensory details:

Dissect what you're seeing; focus on just how many different images make up the scene you're taking in with one glance: sunlight, sky, clouds, trees, sidewalks, grass, buildings, people, cars, animals, utility lines, traffic lights, fire hydrants, mailboxes...on and on. Think about the things you *can't* see: animals hiding in nests, homeless people taking cover, pollen, electronic signals bouncing around in the air.

How many individual noises can you identify? On my walk yesterday, I lost count at 54—traffic noises (engines, horns, stereos), nature noises (birds, wind-blown leaves, dripping water), human noises (yelling, laughing, whistling).

How many scents can you detect? Is the air sweet or pungent? Is that a charcoal grill smoking? *Whew*, that sweaty runner needs a shower!

How many textures can you run your hand over? What kind of surface are you walking on? Is the air cool on your face?

Can you taste the salty sweat on your lips? Stop and get something to eat or drink along the way. Does eating something outside change the taste?

Take a pad of paper with you to record your observations. You will be shocked at how many sensory impressions you'll gather even in a short walk. Use this new awareness to layer detail into your writing.

272. Observation exercise: Insert Yourself

In this observation exercise, you'll make something happen. Look for a chance to insert yourself into a situation in an unobtrusive, unthreatening way. If you see someone drop something, pick it up and return it to them. Offer someone your seat on the train. Smile at someone you pass on the sidewalk. Ask someone for a pen. Watch how the dynamics change as the people around you react to you. Do they ignore you? Welcome you? Reciprocate? Act indifferent? This exercise seems too simple because after all, insertion is what we do every day when we walk out the door, or send an email, or make a phone call. But rarely do we stop to think about how our actions cause reactions or set something in motion, the results of which we might never see.

The insertion exercise makes you more aware of how your characters are supposed to influence and impact each other in big and small ways.

273. Observation exercise: Rewrite the ending

For this exercise, watch a television show or a movie and dissect it. If you were the writer, what would you change? Would you have created different characters, cast the roles differently? What about the setting added to or detracted from the story? How is the pacing, and the length? Does the dialogue progress the story and does it seem authentic? Would you change the ending?

This is a great exercise to do with other people, including non-writers. Caveat: some people say watching a show with a writer is annoying because the writer always sees the twists coming and knows how it will end. Don't be a spoiler! But go ahead and feel smug about your skills as a story-analyzer/fixer.

274. Observation exercise: Create a persona of your reader

To define their target audience, innovative companies create personas representing their range of customers. Creating a persona goes beyond identifying the demographics of a product: single females, ages 18-25, with an income of $25K or less who live in urban environments.

Creating a persona is creating a character who reflects a core segment of your audience. So drawing from the demographic above, a persona might be:

Andrea is a 24-year-old living in metro Atlanta. She works as a travel coordinator for a restaurant management company. She loves her job, but it's stressful and she often works overtime. But Andrea always makes time to run and practice yoga. She enjoys getting out with friends when she can, but in between, they all keep up on social media. Andrea is on the most popular dating website, but she rarely goes out because finding a mate isn't her top priority at the moment. She doesn't own a car, prefers to use public transportation...

Do you see how a vision of a real person begins to emerge? Creating personas forces companies to see their audience not as a blob of faceless customers, but as real people, with real lives and real interests. And it makes them start to consider how and if a customer can work a product into their busy life.

Creating a persona for your target reader can help you envision how a reader will "use" your book to enrich their life. Maybe they need an escape from a harried life. Maybe they'll read your story on their phone while riding the subway. And if they like your book, maybe they'll tell their friends about it.

Now don't you want to write a book for them?

Going through the exercise of creating a persona for your reader is a great reminder you're writing your book for real people to read and react to. If you're willing to take a few minutes to perform this exercise (maybe with your critique group?), it can be so motivating—and clarifying.

275. Observation exercise: The story behind a song

Lyricists are storytellers, too, but they have to be ultra efficient to tell a story and evoke a mood in very few words. Most songs have a beginning, middle, and end, with a repeated chorus in between to tie it all together. Listen to a song and if you don't know/can't make out the lyrics, check the liner notes of the CD/album (hey, I'm old-school), or look them up online. Then make up a story explaining why the songwriter wrote the song and who they wrote it for.

276. Observation exercise: The

story behind a photo

Find a photo in the attic or in an antique store featuring a person/people you don't know, and make up a story about them. Carry the photo around for a while. Give them a name and a background. How do think they felt about the time they were living in? What do you think happened just before the photo was taken, and afterward? Do you think the person is still alive? If not, how do you suppose they might have died?

As with all the observation exercises, this one will simply stimulate those imagination muscles and help you realize the more you spin stories, the better you get at it.

277. Observation exercise: You make up the dialogue

Record a 60-second snippet of a show/movie you're not familiar with and mute the sound; while it's recording, see if you can guess the dialogue simply from the body language of the people in the scene. Jot down notes as you go, then rewind the clip and play the sound to see how close you came.

You can do the same in-person with a couple you can see but not hear... but then you won't know how close you guessed. Still, it's a worthwhile exercise to understand how expression, body position relative to someone else's, and body language can help express an idea or an emotion independent of words. This exercise also illuminates how an unheard (or misheard) conversation and words overheard out of context can be misinterpreted—all fodder for your storytelling skillset.

278. Interval powerhouse workdays

If you're fortunate enough to be able to work on your novel full time, you might be surprised to learn you're as much or more in danger of not finishing your novel as the person who has only a few hours a week to devote to their manuscript. Many writers (me included) find when they have big unstructured blocks of time to write, their page production actually goes down.

To counter the malaise that can set in when writing full time, I've found it helpful to schedule two powerhouse writing days a week. Knowing the 110% effort is short-lived makes it more palatable, and when you see what you can accomplish and how much easier it makes the rest of your week, you might actually start looking forward to it. Are there two days in your week you can kick it up a notch to help you reach your writing goals?

279. Cobble together 30 minutes a day

So you're looking at your schedule of family, work, and social commitments and you're thinking you can't possibly find thirty minutes to work on your novel. But can you reclaim 30 minutes from your day 5 minutes at a time? Can you get up 5 minutes earlier? Shave 5 minutes off the call to your best friend? Steal 5 minutes from your lunch hour? Spend 5 fewer minutes surfing the Internet? Turn away from the television 5 minutes sooner? Go to bed 5 minutes later? That's thirty minutes all together, and 30 minutes is all you need to write 1-2 double-spaced manuscript pages.

280. Accountants vs. writers

My sister is an accountant. Not once has she ever said, "Today I didn't have time to account."

Yet "I don't have time to write," is every writer's ongoing, unending, everlasting, incessant, relentless, annoying lament.

Knock it off. Accountants account, and writers write.

281. Afterglow

Dorothy Parker is attributed with the quote, "I hate writing, I love having written." Writers instantly understand the meaning and the truth behind Parker's quote. As much as you dread sitting down to write a few manuscript pages, the satisfaction in having written them trumps the dread exponentially. Focus on the afterglow of writing, think of how good you're going to feel once you meet your daily or weekly page goal, and let the anticipation of that sweet feeling buoy you along.

282. Watch the pages stack up

I dislike having my picture taken, but I do have one favorite picture from long ago. It's of me sitting at my desk, nearly swallowed up by the stacks of manuscripts I'd written. When I first got into the business, writers needed a reliable, fast printer, and reams of paper to print manuscripts in progress for critique partners, finished manuscripts to submit for publication consideration, and if the book was bought, iterations of revised versions. Paper was our life.

As the publishing industry evolved technologically, editors began to accept email submissions and use track changes in word processing software to process revisions. It wasn't uncommon for one of my books to be released and I suddenly realize I didn't have a printed manuscript for my files.

One thing I miss about the paper days is how gratifying it was to see the sheets of paper stack up as I worked my way through a full manuscript of 350 double-spaced pages. If your novel is trapped in your laptop/tablet, let it out! Print what you've written so far and let the visual proof of your progress push you along.

283. Excuses, excuses

The secret to being a successful *any*thing is to stop making excuses for inertia. DO something toward your goal. Don't talk it to death, and don't think it to death. I know lots of aspiring writers through my local and national writers groups. At least a dozen times a year I have a conversation with an unpublished writer that goes something like this:

Me: "So how's your writing going?"
She: "Oh, you know, about the same. I can't seem to make any progress."
Me: "Have you joined a critique group?"
She: "No, that just takes so much time."
Me: "What about entering contests?"
She: "No, I find the feedback I get from contests so confusing."
Me: "Are you registered for the conference?"
She: "No, I don't have the money."

And on the conversation goes, with me offering ways she can get back on track, and her offering excuses why she can't. And when I see her again a few months later (or the following year), we have basically the same conversation.

It seems as if everyone, not just writers, spends a lot of time making excuses for why they can't follow their dreams. Those same people seem to always be looking for shortcuts. But one surefire shortcut is to cut through the excuses.

284. Make a to-do list every night

When I was in the corporate world, every evening before leaving my office I made a list of things I wanted to tackle the next day. Taking ten minutes to jot down a list helped me to mentally let go of everything knowing I had things teed up for the next day, and the list made each morning less stressful because I didn't waste time trying to figure out where I'd left off the previous day. Making a nightly to-do list is one habit from my corporate life I carried over to my writing life. At the end of every day, I still make a list of things I want to tackle the next day, whether it be pages written, phone calls, promotional activities, or paperwork. And every morning my list helps me get my work day started with a bang!

285. The 10 best pieces of writing
advice *I* ever received: Dialogue

Like most writers, when I hit a snag in my writing, I draw upon inspiration I've received over the course of my career. Recently I started thinking about all those valuable bits of advice imparted in workshops or during personal conversations, and I decided to collect my favorites in one place. I defy you to read the following tips and walk away without at least one kernel of priceless insight!

"I've never encountered a writing dilemma that
couldn't be solved with dialogue."

—Martha Kirkland, author, *Blessings of Mossy Creek*

286. The 10 best pieces of advice *I* ever received: Good vs. great

"The difference between a good book and a great book is typically only a few sentences."

—Annie Jones, author, *The Christmas Sisters*

287. The 10 best pieces of advice

I ever received: Page one

"Show the main character's internal conflict on page one."

—Haywood Smith, author, *Queen Bee Goes Home Again*

288. The 10 best pieces of writing advice *I* ever received: Bestsellers

"Even if you aren't keen on a bestseller, at least try to identify
the universal elements that appealed to so many readers."

—Ruth Kagle, former agent with the Jane Rotrosen Agency, LLC

289. The 10 best pieces of writing advice *I* ever received: Villains

"When it comes to writing villains, ask what emotional, physical or traumatic event triggered this person to commit this act?"

—Rita Herron, author, *All the Beautiful Brides*

290. The 10 best pieces of writing advice *I* ever received: Fire and water

"Write with fire, and let me edit with water."

—Brenda Chin, editor, BelleBooks

291. The 10 best pieces of writing advice *I* ever received: Bad language

"Readers are more forgiving of graphic love scenes or crime scenes than the use of four-letter words; so make your love scenes steamy and your crime scenes gory, but use bad language sparingly."

—*bookseller*

292. The 10 best pieces of writing advice *I* ever received: "Really"

"Give me a 'really' book—really funny, really scary, really sexy, or really emotional."

—Jennifer Enderlin, Senior VP and Publisher, St. Martin's Press

293. The 10 best pieces of writing advice

I ever received: Resolving conflict

"Don't save all the conflict wrap-up for the last few pages; resolving
small conflicts throughout the story is more satisfying to the reader."

—Carmen Green, *That Perfect Moment*

294. The 10 best pieces of writing advice *I* ever received: Hope

"Call it romance, call it literature, call it whatever you want; just write a story that gives me hope, and I'll keep buying."

—*bookstore customer*

295. Imagination drill!

An elderly woman is on her deathbed and reveals a shocking secret to her daughter. What is the secret? Can you think of a scenario for each other following?

The woman's secret is about herself:

The woman's secret is about someone else:

The woman's secret concerns something paranormal:

The woman's secret will send the daughter on a quest:

The woman's secret will affect the entire community:

The woman's secret will affect the entire world:

The woman's secret will change what everyone believes about a historical event:

(For printable PDFs of all Imagination Drills, go to
www.stephaniebond.com.)

296. The 10 worst pieces of writing advice *I* ever received: Synopsis writing

And on the flipside of the best writing advice I've received in my career is…you guessed it: The *worst* writing advice I've received (guilty parties to remain anonymous).

Worst Advice #1: Have someone else write your synopsis. Um, no. In fairness, I believe the thinking behind this one is someone who's objective can sum up your story better than you can. But no—you do the work, then have someone else *read* your synopsis.

297. The 10 worst pieces of writing advice *I* ever received: Chapter vs. scenes

Worst Advice #2: Forget about writing chapters, instead concentrate on writing scenes. Sure, if you have lots of extra time on your hands to go back later and group the scenes into chapters, only to find you need transitions to make them flow seamlessly. File this one under "P" for "Please Make My Life More Complicated."

298. The 10 worst pieces of writing advice

I ever received: Critique groups

Worst Advice #3: Critique groups are dangerous. Not true, unless your critique partners have criminal records. Otherwise, the right critique group will help to keep you motivated and productive. Plus, critiquing other writers' work will make you a stronger writer.

299. The 10 worst pieces of writing advice
I ever received: Book of your heart

Worst Advice #4: Write the book of your heart. Go ahead. Then put a big bow on it and give it to your mother for Christmas, because no one else will be interested in reading it, much less buying it. Then before you begin your second project, analyze your strengths and marry them to the market to find a way to make a sellable idea the book of your heart.

300. The 10 worst pieces of writing advice *I* ever received: Series

Worst Advice #5: Don't pitch a series for your first book. The previous wisdom was an editor will hesitate to buy a series from a new writer because if the first book bombs, the rest of the series is doomed. But editors now recognize a series is the quickest way to build readership, so if you have a good idea for a series, go for it.

301. The 10 worst pieces of writing
advice *I* ever received: Editing

Worst Advice #6: Don't allow an editor to change your work. *Wrong.* Remember, you're writing for a worldwide audience—let your editor do her job as long as she isn't nitpicking your work to death. She just might be making your work more sellable to other, far-reaching markets.

302. The 10 worst pieces of writing advice
I ever received: Editor relationship

Worst Advice #7: Don't befriend your editor. Wrong again. It's not a good idea to become best-buddy confidantes, but you should strive for a professional friendship with your editor. This industry is complicated and frustrating—it's always nice if you're conducting business with someone you actually like, and vice versa. An editor who champions your work to industry professionals you might not have access to is priceless.

303. The 10 worst pieces of writing advice *I* ever received: Rules

Worst Advice #8: Writing rules are made to be broken. Actually, no, they're not. It's true some writers have broken out by breaking the rules, but those success stories are mostly anecdotal. The straightest path to success is following the rules, especially on your first novel. Once you get your writing legs under you, then you can go rogue if you want. But once you get your writing legs under you, you'll better appreciate the value of rules.

304. The 10 worst pieces of writing advice

I ever received: Self-promotion

Worst Advice #9: Self-promotion is useless. This statement is mostly wrong. Self-promotion without purpose can be a waste of time and money, but if you plan a self-promotion campaign wisely, you can influence a certain percentage of your sales. There are some promotional activities an author can simply do better than a publishing house (a website, for example). But don't put yourself in financial jeopardy to promote your book.

305. The 10 worst pieces of writing advice *I* ever received: Font size

Worst Advice #10: Use a larger font—your editor will never know you skimped on wordcount. Unless she looks at the bottom of her word processing software screen where it lists the wordcount of the manuscript she's reading/editing.

306. Imagination drill!

Your character is stranded on a deserted tropical island with trees and vegetation for one year. There is no cell service, so electronic communication is out of the question, as is any means of escape. He/she is wearing jeans, a T-shirt, a sweatshirt, socks, and running shoes. They have all the raw fish and seaweed they can eat, so they won't starve. You can give him/her 10 individual items for protection, tools, entertainment, etc. for the one year. What 10 items do you choose?

1.

2.

3.

4.

5.

6.

7.

8.

9.

10.

(For printable PDFs of all Imagination Drills, go to
www.stephaniebond.com.)

307. Coach's confessions:

10 things I wish I'd known, #1

For writers, hindsight is 20/40 (because most of us have wrecked our eyesight by staring at computer screens). I don't have any big regrets, but looking back, there are a few things I wish I'd known earlier in my career. I'm sharing 10 tidbits with you:

I wish I'd known to use a pen name. My given name is a good writing name, so I chose to use it. I didn't foresee the proliferation of social media and online communication/transactions. It's difficult, if not impossible, to keep my private Stephanie Bond accounts and interactions separate from my business Stephanie Bond accounts and interactions. There are times when I'd like a little more anonymity.

308. Coach's confessions:

10 Things I wish I'd known, #2

I wish I'd known to link every book to a previous book somehow. I did it haphazardly, when my editor and I planned it, but even if books aren't formally tied together in a series, there are ways to plant "Easter eggs" for your readers, little treats of tie-in details, cameo characters or crossover settings that only your avid followers pick up on. It's fun for you and for your readers, and any time you can inject fun into the writing process, do it!

309. Coach's confessions:
10 things I wish I'd known, #3

Speaking of linked books, I wish I'd started writing series earlier in my career. Back then publishers pushed standalone books; they didn't want to commit to a multi-book series in case the first book flopped. But I wish I'd pushed harder. Readers love series and it makes a writer's job easier, too.

310. Coach's confessions:
10 Things I wish I'd known, #4

When I started writing, long, chunky paperbacks were popular. It wasn't uncommon for publishers to request 120,000-150,000 words (that's 480-600 manuscript pages). When paper prices rose and wordcounts were cut to 100,000, writers felt as if we were being penalized. Now wordcounts for full-length novels are around 90,000 words, and a large segment of readers prefer even shorter books. I couldn't have known the proliferation of e-readers and phones combined with shorter attention spans would pull wordcounts lower and lower, but I wish I'd known. I would've written shorter books, and released more titles.

311. Coach's confessions:
10 Things I wish I'd known, #5

I've been a prolific writer most of my career, releasing 3-4 novels a year, and sometimes more. In hindsight, I wish I'd built in more downtime between books. When I think back to the year I wrote 8 projects, I'm not sure how I kept my sanity because while I was writing one book, I'd be revising another, approving copyedits on yet another, and reading page proofs on still another. I remember referring to that year as my "Year of Writing Dangerously"! At the end of it, I was completely burnt out.

312. Coach's confessions:

10 Things I wish I'd known, #6

I wish I'd known not to commit to projects too far into the future. At the time, the lifecycle of creating a book was 12-18 months, so a 3-book contract could mean committing to four years into the future. That's too long considering how quickly the industry began to change, and is still changing.

313. Coach's confessions:

10 Things I wish I'd known, #7

In hindsight, I wish I'd known not to plan deadlines around personal holidays. Inevitably, I would have to choose between missing birthday celebrations or other special occasions and sending in my book late.

314. Coach's confessions:

10 Things I wish I'd known, #8

I wish I'd known my editor had no idea how much money my books earned. Editors sometimes get sales information, but they don't generally see royalty statements. So while they might have an idea of how many copies of the book sold, they typically don't know how much a title earns over its lifetime, neither for the publisher nor for the author. It's one of the stranger parts of a somewhat obscure industry and business model.

315. Coach's confessions:

10 Things I wish I'd known, #9

In hindsight, I wished I'd known more about copyright law. Copyrights don't have to be registered, but an author has more protection if they are; some publishers will register the copyright on your behalf, some don't. And there are specific rules about copyright reversion every author should know. The good news is you don't need an attorney to be informed—all the information is online now. Take a few minutes to read up on copyrights, if only to file it under "Good to Know."

316. Coach's confessions:
10 Things I wish I'd known, #10

In hindsight, I've written so many novels, the novelty wore off, so to speak. I'm not referring to the content—I love all the books I've written; I mean the novelty of *finishing* a book wore off. I wish I'd stopped to celebrate each book with a bottle of champagne and a tattoo. Okay, maybe not a tattoo, but you get the gist. Writing a complete novel is a big honking deal, and it deserves to be rejoiced, even if it's a one-person party! (Recently I've started buying charms for each book I finish, something that reminds me of the book, and I've started going back to buy charms for all my early titles.)

GETTING TO THE FINISH LINE

Don't quit now—finish strong!

317. How do you know when your story is done?

You know the feeling you get when you're sitting in a movie and you're thinking, *This movie should've ended twenty minutes ago*? Yeah, *that* feeling. That's how you know when your story is done, when it's starting to wear out its welcome. If you have critique partners, they'll let you know when your story is done—or should be—because they'll be ready for it to end, too. Are your characters starting to seem tired or become repetitive? Do they bicker with each other on the page? That's because they're also ready for you to wrap it up. You've reached the beginning of the end...in a good way.

318. Give the end its due

One of the hardest aspects of writing a book is devising an appropriate ending. If you didn't plan an ending in your synopsis in the hope that something would occur to you in the writing of the book (and it didn't), stop now and figure it out, keeping the following in mind:

- The ending should be crafted just as carefully as every other plot point in your novel.
- The ending represents the culmination of all your hard work.
- The ending is the character's reward, and the reader's reward. (And yours!)
- The ending should measure up to the quality of the rest of your novel.
- The ending is the last thing the reader will remember.
- The ending can wreck a good story, or redeem a so-so story.

319. Reader payoff

When it comes to movies, I believe most of them fall down/come up short in the category of reader payoff. When you hear someone say, "It was okay, could've been better," it usually means they hung in there until the end, but were ultimately disappointed—they didn't get the payoff they were expecting for the time and/or money they invested. Don't pull your reader all the way to the end of a romance and not give them a memorable declaration of love. Don't drag your reader through a fast-paced quest for a treasure and not show the scene where the gold is discovered. Don't scare the socks off your reader with an otherworldly entity and not explain why it chose your character to harass. Don't get so caught up in ending your book you forget to give the reader what they paid for.

320. Over-deliver on the ending

Along the lines of reader payoff, keep in mind an over-delivered ending is better than a rushed ending. In previous segments I mentioned how one or two sentences can make a big difference in satisfying the reader. The ending is one of the places in your story where one or two sentences can make *all* the difference. This is one section where you can be a little melodramatic. Push for bigger emotion/drama than feels comfortable—if it seems a little over the top, it's okay. Go for the gut (and the heart) in those last few pages!

321. Ways to end your novel

Of course there are many ways to end your novel, but here are a few tried and true methods:

The full circle ending—Place your character(s) in the same situation as an earlier scene, but this time they behave differently. For example, she's a workaholic who would answer her phone at all hours, to the detriment of personal relationships. So maybe at the end, her phone rings and we see her simply reach into her purse and turn it off.

The "satisfying" ending—The satisfying ending is short of happily ever after. Everything gets tied up, but the story doesn't have a storybook ending. An example of a satisfying ending is when a character dies, but is at peace when they take their last breath.

The twist ending—In the twist ending, everything the reader has been led to believe up to that point is turned on end. Perhaps a good guy turns out to be a bad guy, or the story is taking place only in the character's mind.

The "to be continued" ending—In this ending, you let the reader know the characters will live on after the book ends. For instance, if you're writing a romance novel and your characters are together at the end, it's great if one of them proposes and the other one accepts…but maybe the next line from the hero is, "You're going to love my mom," and the heroine gives him a frozen smile because she has a feeling she won't. You've given them a happy ending, but the reader will be even happier to close the book knowing the characters are off on another adventure (in her mind).

322. A word about twist endings

Readers love twist endings—with caveats. A twist ending can't violate the rules of the genre, i.e., the hero/heroine in a romance aren't supposed to die. Also, some justice must be served; if, for example the villain gets away, perhaps he is allowed to escape after he gives up the location of a kidnapped child. Horror novels/movies can get away with twist endings because their purpose is to unnerve you. But a twist ending has to make sense—it should leave the reader saying, "*Wow!*" instead of "*Huh?*"

323. The last line of your novel

Just as the first line of your novel should resonate with tone, so should the last line of your novel. If you've written a romantic comedy, consider making the last line funny. If you've written a coming of age story, the last line should vibrate with youthful wisdom. Pick a few novels from your bookshelf and turn to the last line—do you get a sense of the tone of the story that was just told? Movies are another great source of last lines—every movie maker strives to end a film memorably. When I discussed plotting your novel, I mentioned at the end of the story, your character's world should be changed, or they should see their world differently. So if you're stuck for a last line, consider falling back on dialogue and let one of your characters say something to sum up where the story has led them.

324. The ending as a punctuation mark

I like to think of my ending scene(s) collectively as a punctuation mark at the end of a very long sentence. Is the ending an ellipsis—does it lead the reader into a sigh? Or is it a period—does it tie up all the loose ends in a pretty bow? Or is it a question mark—does it leave the reader wondering what's next for the character? Or is it an exclamation point—does it make the reader gasp? If you're going for a final emotional punch, visualizing your ending as a punctuation mark will help you *hit* the mark.

325. Countdown to the end

Are you the type of person who is motivated by the work you've already accomplished, or by the work you have left to do? While I'm working on a manuscript, I keep a spreadsheet of pages written per chapter, which not only gives me a running total of pages I've finished, but also pages left until I reach my goal. Toward the end of my manuscript, I'm *always* more motivated by the "pages until goal" number! If counting down to the end motivates you, use counters or big red X's or other visual cues to help you get to the finish line.

326. What if your book won't end?

You can't just assume your story is going to tie itself up. *You* have to end it, else it will just keep unspooling, like a never ending story. With nearly every project, my friends and I joke when we're at the "bomb" point—that means we're at the point where we want to write, "And then a bomb went off, and everyone died. The End." We've all been there.

But of course, you have to finish what you started! What if you settled in to read a book and got 300 pages in only to find a note that read "At this point, the author lost interest in the story and quit. Sorry."

327. What's stopping you?

There are many reasons why writers can't bring their manuscripts to a close. Perhaps they've written themselves into a corner they can't get out of. Or they've presented too many problems and can't get everything tied up in the pagecount they have left.

But generally, the reasons novels don't reach The End lie more in mental or emotional blocks. If you can't make yourself sit down and finish a manuscript, something is stopping you. You're getting some kind of payoff by not completing your novel. Is it the pleasure of watching television or shopping when you know you should be writing because you love the feeling of getting away with something? Is it the thrill of the adrenaline rush when you have to finish a book under pressure? Is it the attention you get when you lament to friends and family that you're suffering from writer's block? Or, if you're unpublished, is it the comfort of knowing if you never finish a manuscript, you won't have to submit it to a publisher and face possible rejection?

328. Fear of failure/fear of success

So you want to be a novelist—or you thought you did. But now that your novel is almost done, the nerves are setting in. All those people who've been asking how the book is coming along are now going to be asking if anyone has bought it yet. It's a lot more fun to tell everyone at a party you're *writing* a novel than to tell everyone you've *written* a novel, but no one wants it. One way to keep pushing that problem farther into the future is simply to postpone ending your novel.

Many writers suffer from a fear of failure or a fear of success. The writing of their novel is something they can control. But submitting a novel to a publisher or self-publishing it means opening yourself and your beloved book to possible criticism, and that's completely out of your control. If you're having qualms that finishing your novel will plunge you into unknown, scary waters, you're completely normal. But you simply have to get over it. Because a great manuscript that never sees the light of day is the same as the manuscript that was never begun.

329. Finally, The End

When I finish writing a manuscript, the euphoria is so complete, I wish I could bottle the feeling and sell *it* instead of the book! For a writer, the words "The End" are two of the most wonderful words in the dictionary. I have my own "signature"—I put a hyphen on either side, bold it, and center it like this:

-The End-

I think that's pretty reserved considering what I'd like to do, which is:

THE END!!!

(For the record, the line editor or the copy editor will put a line through the words to delete them so they won't appear in the actual book, but besides being satisfying, I like to write "The End" so no one in the interminable production process has to worry if somehow the last page of the manuscript got lost along the way.)

330. The emotional lifecycle of writing a novel

I have a friend who is in the throes of finishing a book—when you're in the middle of it yourself, you don't realize how manic those last few days can be. Talking to her made me think about the emotional lifecycle of writing a novel:

In the beginning, everything is new and fun—you can write for hours and not realize how much time has passed. Slowly, the novelty wears off, and the writing becomes harder—maybe you're not sure what to do next. But if you have faith in the story and the discipline to keep pushing, you typically get past that initial hump...only to run into another roadblock, usually about every 3 or 4 chapters.

At some point, you think you just can't do it, that you were never meant to be a writer and your editor, if she is desperate and accepts this manuscript, will certainly never buy another book from you. Then you remember you felt this way about every book you've written at a certain point. And you have to trust yourself and hope you know enough about what you're doing that the manuscript doesn't seem as fragmented, episodic, boring, hoaky, and melodramatic to your editor as it seems to you.

Those last few days of meeting a deadline are an emotional rollercoaster—you're exhausted, but you need to keep working and strangely, you might find you do your best work under pressure. Your body is crying out for sleep, but you have so much adrenaline pumping through your veins you couldn't possibly rest. When you're finally finished, you're so relieved you call every other writer you know because only another writer truly understands how wonderful that feeling is.

Then you start thinking about the next book!

331. The bones of a book

One part of putting a book together is assembling what I call the "bones" of a book. Sure, you have the story which is the most important part, but there are other parts of a book that help to hold it together, give the reader a full reading experience, and give the author the most exposure possible. These pieces of information are also known as the "front matter" or the "back matter" depending on if they appear before the story or after. If you submit your manuscript to a traditional publisher and it's accepted for publication, your editor might ask you to supply information to help build the front and back matter. If you decide to self-publish your book, it's good to know what some of those sections are called.

332. The bones of a book: Foreword

A foreword is typically associated more often with nonfiction books, sometimes as a note from the author as to the genesis of the book, or perhaps written by another person to lend support or credibility to the book. Most readers don't like or read forewords, which is why in the front of this book, I labeled the "foreword" section "Read this first." (Else, you wouldn't have read it, would you?) In a novel, the foreword would be replaced by either a letter from the author or perhaps a note from the editor or publisher.

333. The bones of a book: Acknowledgements

The acknowledgements sections of a book is optional and written by the author to thank people who contributed to the creation of the book in some way—perhaps they inspired you to write the book, or have made a difference in your life, or provided moral support while you were writing the book. This is also the section where most authors thank their agent or editor or anyone else who helped to get the book to the point of publication, such as research sources. You can thank anyone you want, but try to keep this section as brief as possible.

334. The bones of a book: Dedication

The dedication of a novel is also optional and also left up to the author as to who to mention. The dedication is more personal and is a nice way to spotlight people who have played a special role in your life. Some authors mention a cause here, especially if the cause is mentioned in the book. I've dedicated books to members of my family, my editor, and even to nameless groups, such as "This book is dedicated to everyone who has an old flame they can't forget" or something similar.

335. The bones of a book: Author letter

I like to include a letter from the author section. My publishers put this section in the front matter, but in my self-published books, I put this section in the back matter. In the letter from the author, I always thank my readers for buying and reading my book, and tell them something about the writing of the book—perhaps where the idea came from, or issues that came up while I was writing it. I also invite readers to drop by my website and sign up for my mailing list. A letter from author is a nice, simple way to connect with readers.

336. The bones of a book: Author bio

It's a good idea to include an author bio and a picture if you have one you'd like to use. Readers are eager to know something about you. Your bio doesn't have to read like a eulogy—it should reflect your personality. It's always nice to mention your background and maybe something about what got you interested in writing or your hobbies. Many authors mention if they're a parent or grandparent, or the master of a beloved pet. And some authors include what part of the world they live in. Again, this is another chance for you to connect with readers.

337. The bones of a book: Extras

Depending on what type of story you write, you might consider including extras for the reader to enhance the understanding of the story. For example, if your story features a special dialect or vocabulary that's unfamiliar to the public at large, you might want to include a list of words and their meaning for readers to refer to. If your story is a saga about a multi-generational family, you might want to include a family tree. If your story is set in a fictional world/galaxy, you might include a map or a description of the world. Extras are just that—bonus features that contribute to a value-added reading experience.

338. Imagination drill!

This drill is about cause and effect and how the smallest of actions can set off unforeseen reactions.

A man walks into a drycleaners to pick up a jacket he needs for a presentation that day. The man working the counter says the jacket isn't ready.

1. The customer yells at the man and causes a scene, then walks out.
2. The man at the counter turns around and kicks his dog.
3. The dog

Can you finish the third interaction and 7 more, all escalating in negativity/severity? (Bonus points if the last interaction involves the original customer!)

4.

5.

6.

7.

8.

9.

10.

(For printable PDFs of all Imagination Drills, go to
www.stephaniebond.com.)

POST GAME

Scoring is all about follow-through!

339. Submitting your novel

The good news is your novel is finally written! The bad news is there are lots of decisions to make under the heading of "What now?":

- Where should I send my novel?
- Which editor within the publishing house should I send it to?
- What exactly do I send?
- How long until I receive a response?
- Do I need an agent? (Which brings up another set of questions.)

Now the research begins. If you've attended conferences and writing group meetings, you might already have an idea of where you'd like to submit your book. Fortunately, publishers post their submission guidelines on their websites, so research is easier now. The standard of exhaustive publisher (and agent) listings is the *Writer's Market* published by *Writer's Digest*. If you belong to a national writing organization, the organization probably maintains an "approved" list of publishers and agents who are looking for manuscripts.

340. Do you need an agent?

The agent question is always sticky. The short answer is *no*, you don't need an agent to get your book published (and certainly not if you decide to self-publish). But if your goal is to be published long-term by a traditional publisher, then the answer changes to *probably, at some point*. You'll generally get better access to editors and more money if you have an agent. And some publishers don't accept unagented manuscripts. But be aware, securing an agent can be a long, laborious process in and of itself. In fact, it's more difficult to find an agent who will take you on than to find an editor who will take you on. An editor is willing to take a chance you're a one-book wonder; but an agent, whose income depends on their clients' income, has to be sure you're in this for the long haul.

Another tactic is to wait until you have an offer from a publisher before contacting agents, but then you lose out on a lot of what an agent should be doing for you in the first place.

If you want to work with an agent, my general advice is to wait until you receive "good" rejection letters from editors (yes, there are such things as good rejection letters) before approaching agents to demonstrate your material is close to being accepted.

341. What to include in your

submission package

When you're ready to query an agent or publisher, check the company's website to see what they're currently looking for (third-party online and printed listings might be out of date).

If a query letter only is requested: Your query letter should explain your idea and something about you, 2 pages max. You should mail it in a regular #10 envelope, or, if the guidelines say it's okay, many publishers/agencies accept queries via e-mail.

If a proposal or "sample chapters" or "partial manuscript" is requested: Send a query letter describing your project and you (again, 2 pages max), a separate short synopsis of your manuscript (1-2 pages), and the *first* 3 chapters. ("Sample chapters" doesn't mean chapters 1, 15, and 30.)

If a full manuscript has been requested: Send a query letter, a short synopsis, and a full hardcopy of the manuscript (unless the publisher/agency accepts submission via e-mail and you'd rather go that route).

If you submit a printed copy of a manuscript (either a partial or a full), you need to become intimately acquainted with the term "SASE": self-addressed stamped envelope. When you submit material via snail mail, you should always include an SASE with enough stamped postage to cover its return to you.

342. More DOs and DON'Ts of

submitting your novel

DO try to find the name of a specific editor and their title to submit your material to.

DON'T use colored paper—white only, 20 lb. (anything heavier will jam some copiers).

DON'T bind a printed manuscript; to keep it together, use a large rubber band.

DON'T send the material in a manner that has to be signed for (unless the editor asks you to send it guaranteed delivery); you can get delivery confirmation through the postal service without having to obtain a signature.

DON'T include extraneous material such as pictures of your characters and/or the names of actors whom you believe should play your characters when your book is optioned for a movie.

DON'T try to be cute by including glitter bombs—or cash!

DO follow protocol and be professional.

343. Write an effective query letter

An effective query letter should contain all the following pieces of information in 2 pages or less:

- your name and contact information
- the title of your project
- wordcount of your project
- description of your project
- what you're offering (a proposal? the complete manuscript?)
- your credentials

Sounds easy enough, right? Until you sit down and try to squeeze all the information into a few paragraphs. On top of everything else, you're trying to convince the editor/agent to request your material, so your letter has to be...well, *interesting*. Like a little infomercial. There's no standard format for a query letter—just be professional, brief, and fascinating.

344. Top reasons query letters fail

- letter is too long
- description of project is unclear
- author doesn't mention wordcount
- author doesn't mention if project is complete
- letter is too long
- author says it took ten years to write the manuscript
- author indicates this is the first book in a twenty-seven book series
- letter is too long
- author mentions the idea for the book came from a dead relative who appeared to them in a dream
- author sounds unstable (see previous item)
- writer doesn't go for "the close" (May I send you the full manuscript?)
- letter is TOO LONG

Okay, the above list is a little tongue-in-cheek, but you get the gist. I emphasize the length of your query letter because the person reading your material has a stack of submissions to get through. The more succinct your submission, the greater the chance of it being read and responded to versus being shuffled to the bottom of the reading pile.

When you write your query letter, be clear, be thorough, be brief, and don't sound like a kook.

345. Waiting game

How long will it take to get a response from your query or submission? Most publishers and agents will list response time in their guidelines. Whatever time is given, double it. Mark the day on your calendar to follow up, and turn your attention elsewhere.

SO much of a writer's time is spent waiting, especially in the beginning. But even after selling that first book, or even after selling the first *few* books, there will always be waiting—waiting to hear back from your agent or editor about a new idea you have, waiting to hear if a manuscript has been approved, waiting to hear if an offer will be forthcoming for a new contract, waiting to hear if sales are satisfactory, waiting to hear if subsidiary opportunities (such as audio or foreign language sales) will ever materialize.

Some of the "hurry up and wait" element of this business is because so many different people have to weigh in on/contribute to a book project, it's logistically difficult to align so many schedules for a committee decision to actually be made and then delivered back to you.

What's a writer to do? Find ways to stay busy. *Always* be working ahead. Don't let a stalled decision stall your work schedule. Always have extra projects in the wings. Always have a plan B. No matter what happens, keep moving forward. Start writing a new novel. Then if you get an offer for your first novel, you'll already have a second novel underway to offer up as well.

346. Dealing with rejection

Most (all) writers are crushed when they receive their first rejection letter. Some are so crushed they abandon their fledgling writing career altogether. But to make it in this business, you can't take rejection so personally. Sure, it feels personal because your manuscript is your creation. So if someone doesn't like your novel enough to buy it, it feels as if they don't like *you* enough to buy it. Which simply isn't true. A rejection could mean your manuscript isn't ready. Or it could mean it isn't right for that person. Or maybe they like it, but they bought a similar manuscript last week.

Think about it this way: Say you're at an art fair with booths and booths of handcrafted jewelry, clothing, sculpture, etc., with the intent of buying gifts for all your friends. But you have only $500 in your pocket, and your friends have unique and varied tastes that might or might not reflect what you like. So you go up and down the aisles, shopping for the best buys for your budget and your needs. Just because you don't buy something doesn't mean you don't like it—and it absolutely doesn't mean you don't like the person who made it! That's how it is for editors—they have to buy for a wide audience, and they only have so much money to spend. They can't buy everything, and if they don't buy your manuscript, it doesn't mean they're rejecting *you*. Keep trying.

347. Evaluating a rejection letter

If you're fortunate enough to receive a personal rejection letter (versus a form rejection letter), take some time to process the disappointment. Then take some time to analyze what the agent or editor said about your submission. The more detailed the feedback, the more likely the person will read your submission again if you decide to make the suggested changes. A big pet peeve of agents and editors is when they invest time in reading a submission and giving specific feedback for improvement, then the writer makes the changes and sends it somewhere else!

By the way, I never received a "good" rejection letter when I was trying to break into the business. So even if you receive a form rejection letter with faded print that's skewed on the sheet of paper because it's been photocopied so many times, there's still hope.

348. Should you self-publish?

When I got into the publishing business, there was no choice except to go the traditional route through New York publishers. Print books ruled; eBooks were still years away. In 2011, I self-published a dozen novels I'd gotten the rights back to over the years, while I still had traditional publishing contracts to fulfill. So for a while, I had a foot in both sides of the industry. Now I'm mostly self-published, although I continue to have hybrid projects for which some of the rights are being independently exercised, and some of the rights are being managed by traditional publishers. Each situation has its advantages, depending on your goals and your time constraints.

The unanswerable question is determining which type of publishing will earn you the most money. With self-publishing, you'll earn more for each copy sold. With traditional publishing, you won't earn as much for each copy sold, but the book will probably (although not always) achieve wider distribution and sell more copies overall. Which is more important to you?

349. The pros of self-publishing your first novel

- You don't have to endure the protracted submission process to traditional publishers.
- You will have total control over your content, cover, release date, and price.
- You can release books as soon as and as often as you write them.
- You can respond to reader feedback more quickly.
- You can change/update your book and republish at any time.
- Your royalties are paid every month.
- You retain all rights.

If your book sells well, you can still submit a proposal to an agent and/or publisher, with sales data to prove your book is being well-received by readers.

350. The cons of self-publishing your first novel

- You won't see your name on the book on a bookstore bookshelf. (Although you can make your book available in print through print-on-demand services.)
- You won't receive an advance payment on your book.
- You have total control of the content, cover, release date, and price—it's all on you.
- You will need some technical skills.
- You will have to exercise subsidiary rights (audio, foreign language) on your own.
- You will have to divide your time between writing, administrative tasks, marketing…and a thousand other bits and pieces.

Note: I include a book on self-publishing in the recommended books section at the end.

351. Do you know how lucky you are?

If you think writing a novel today is hard, consider what writers throughout history had to work with: Sticks, bones, feather quills, lead pencils, metal pen points and ink, ball point pens, and manual typewriters...for printing on "paper" than ranged from dirt to stone to hides to papyrus to wax tablets to handmade pulp. Today we have laptops with intuitive word processing software that deduces what words we're typing, makes suggestions, corrects spelling, and flags questionable grammar. We can italicize, bold, and add other formatting with a swipe, plus write in an array of fonts, at any size and in any color. A thesaurus and dictionary are only a click away. And when you're finished writing your novel, you can even publish the book yourself if you choose to and start earning royalties instantly.

Seriously, how much easier do you want it?

352. Rinse and repeat

When you finish your novel, do take time to celebrate your achievement. But I encourage you to get started on another project as soon as possible, while you're in the habit of writing. I like to get back to work quickly to take advantage of the momentum and adrenaline of finishing a book. (Although I will definitely start writing the new novel at a slower pace.) One reason I keep going is I know my next book is going to help sell the book I just completed. The best promotional tool at a writer's disposal is simply to get more inventory out there. The more projects you have available, the better the chances readers will find you. And if they like what they read, they'll give your other books a try. With that in mind, the best way to sell book 1 is to write and publish book 2. And the best way to sell book 2 is to write and publish book 3…and so on.

353. The cumulative effect

Occasionally you'll hear about a new author who experiences stratospheric success with his or her first novel. Those stories make some people believe if they write a book and put it out there, readers will come in droves. And they might—I certainly hope it happens for you! But if it doesn't, keep in mind most writers labor for years before they experience real success, and it's usually not on the first book or the third or the fifth. Sometimes the eighth book or the eleventh is the tipping point of a career, and the author becomes a success when readers discover they have a deep backlist.

In my experience, much of a writer's success is due to a cumulative effect of building a readership book by book, and building a cohesive body of work that becomes a recognizable brand simply because the stories are all told in your unique voice. Too often novelists give up if they don't experience bestsellerdom right out of the gate. If they perceive their first novel as a failure, to write a second novel seems counterintuitive, yet that's exactly what they should do. If your first novel isn't the raging success you hoped it would be, I hope you'll be patient and keep writing until the cumulative effect kicks in.

354. Familiar fiction

If you decide to keep writing after your first novel is finished (and I hope you do!), be aware the first few stories will come to you more easily in a phase I call "familiar fiction." In the familiar fiction phase, you usually write about things from your own experiences. You draw from childhood memories and family dysfunction, friendships you've found and lost, first kisses and failed romances, coming of age and growing cynical. Eventually, however, those closely-held references will be exhausted, forcing you to reach farther, dig deeper, and tap into your imagination to come up with new stories. Moving past the familiar fiction phase is where you begin to grow by leaps and bounds as a writer because you will realize just how elastic your mind can be.

COACHING CASE STUDIES

I've aggregated the hundreds of writers' personalities and issues I've encountered during my career into the following archetypes. Do you recognize yourself among them?

355. Coaching case study: Can't-Finish Carl

Carl loves writing! He writes more pages than anyone in his writing group. The problem is, he can't seem to ever finish a project. Carl is always working on a new idea that's better than his last idea. THIS idea is THE ONE he tells his writing group. But this idea is like all the others—only as promising as the person who's writing it. Sure enough, the following week, Carl discards the idea for yet another.

Assessment: Carl loves the thrill of the chase. He thrives on the excitement of something new, and the potential of an untapped idea. But at the first sign of the hard work ahead to bring the idea to fruition, Carl assumes the idea is flawed and discards it in favor of another idea.

Recommendation: Carl needs to suspend all further ideas until he takes one to completion. And he might be better suited to writing short-form fiction rather than a full-length novel. Writing short stories and novellas would give Carl the quick fix he needs and allow him to keep pursuing the next good idea.

356. Coaching case study:

Sophomore-Slump Susie

Susie made a splash when she joined her local writing group. When she presented her idea for a novel, everyone agreed it was a winner. The title was fantastic and memorable—the kind of title everyone wished they'd thought of. She wrote the first few chapters and entered them into various contests. She won lots of prizes and editors who judged asked her to send them the book when it was finished. Everywhere Susie went, people remember her book and ask about it. Year...after year...after year. After six years she finally finished writing the book and sold it to her first-choice editor in a two-book contract. The first book needed no revisions, so Susie was able to get to work on the second book right away. Except she can't seem to get going...and no way is she going to meet her deadline.

Assessment: Susie wrote a splendid first book because she had all the time in the world to plan it, ruminate, tweak it, add to it, layer in subplots, get feedback from every contest and every writer in her group, polish it, and make it perfect. She poured everything she had into that book...and now she doesn't seem to have anything left. Susie is suffering from Sophomore Slump; deep down she's afraid her second book could never measure up to her first book, so she can't seem to get started on it.

Recommendation: Susie needs to accept the fact that every novel she writes will be different; some books will simply be "better" than others, or will sell better because of their subject matter, cover, price, etc. She should plow ahead on book two and make it as good as she can in the timeframe she has. She might surprise herself and realize she doesn't have to massage a book for six years in order to turn out a really decent, entertaining novel.

357. Coaching case study: Help-Me Helen

Helen is a really good writer. She's sold several books to a major publisher and her career seems to be going well. But her critique partners have begun to dread the weekly meetings; instead of turning in pages to be critiqued, Helen asks her group to help her plot the next few scenes in the book she's working on. Her critique group is happy to brainstorm plot movements when members hit a snag in their stories, but Helen relies on the group to plot her entire book for her. Worse, when she sends her manuscripts to her editor, she leaves gaping holes with handwritten notes to her editor that read "I don't know what to do here—do you have any ideas?"

Assessment: Helen has grown dependent on others, either out of laziness or a lack of confidence. And consciously or sub-consciously, it's also an attention-getting ploy; Helen feels loved when people are helping her.

Recommendation: Helen needs to find her independence. Her critique group should insist all members bring detailed synopses or chapter outlines of their books before they begin writing chapters. By forcing Helen to do the hard work up front, they will circumvent her reliance on them. In the process, hopefully Helen will realize the book will go more smoothly if she plans it beforehand...which will build her self-confidence.

358. Coaching case study: Hang-On Hannah

Hannah has a great idea—er, make that *had* a great idea. Three years ago. She wrote a really decent manuscript about a cowboy hero named Deacon that made the editorial rounds. The feedback was mostly good, but editors said it fell just short of being strong enough to buy, and they all passed. Hannah had other plans. She decided to rewrite the book and make Deacon an FBI agent. When it still didn't sell, she rewrote it with Deacon as a vampire...

Assessment: It's one thing to be invested in your characters, but Hannah can't let go of Deacon. It's a little creepy.

Recommendation: Hannah needs to move on! In the time she's spent on this manuscript, she could've had three manuscripts to show for it, which would increase her chances of selling at least one of them. It's okay to fall in love with your characters, but not if it impedes you as a writer. It's better to get those books out there so *other* people can fall in love with your characters!

359. Coaching case study: Stroke-Me Sam

Sam is a great writer. He's written several books for reputable publishers, but he has a problem getting his books turned in on time. His first editor was patient because she loved Sam's writing. She showered him with compliments and when his confidence waned, she always propped him back up. Sam loved the accolades, so he was careful not to send in material unless it was perfect. Then his editor changed jobs and Sam was assigned a different editor. His new editor also likes his writing, but she's more hands-off—and less patient about missed deadlines. She's threatening not to buy another book from him if he doesn't change his ways.

Assessment: Sam is a perfectionist who's afraid to send in anything he thinks isn't up to snuff. He doesn't want to disappoint his editor so he revises and polishes until he misses his deadlines. He sees his new editor's aloofness as rejection, which makes him shut down.

Recommendation: Sam should realize he's going to have many editors over his career, and he can't expect them all to take the time to stroke him—they have lots of other writers to manage. Sam needs to become a more mature, low-maintenance writer. If he would turn in his manuscripts on time but less than perfect, his editor would be happier. Plus it would give her the chance to provide feedback for revisions that would make her more invested in his book.

360. Coaching case study: Freebie Faye

Faye is a good writer, but she can't seem to get any traction. Editors have invited her to contribute to round robin stories on their websites and charitable (nonpaid) story collections with the promise of visibility. And she's sold a few short stories to confession magazines in return for copies of the magazine. She recently banded with a group of self-published authors to put out a boxed set of eBooks at 99 cents just to get her name out there. The boxed set sold a few hundred copies, but with the small royalty for each copy being divided 12 ways, she hasn't yet recouped the money she pitched in to buy ads. Which, now that she thinks about it, isn't going to benefit her anyway because even if readers like her story, she doesn't have another book for them to buy.

Assessment: Faye is being reactive to every offer that comes her way, and she doesn't put enough value on her work. And if Faye doesn't value her work, no one else will.

Recommendation: If Faye's top priority is to get her books into the hands of as many readers as possible, then there's no problem. But if Faye is seeking an income stream, she should pause to plan her next career move. Write a novel to self-publish at regular price or to sell to a traditional publisher, then use the freebie/inexpensive projects to push readers toward the higher-revenue project.

361. Coaching case study: Social Seth

Seth is the life of the writing group. He's been an officer every year since he joined, organizes the local conference, and supports every event. He's every member's biggest cheerleader and buys everyone's books when they're published. Everyone loves Seth. But he doesn't write much anymore. In fact, he still hasn't finished writing the manuscript that won an award for Best Opening Scene a few year ago. So when the writing group's parent organization changes its membership guidelines to require members to provide proof they're seriously pursuing a writing career by submitting a full-length manuscript, Seth gets defensive.

Assessment: Seth likes the *idea* of being a writer more than actually being a writer.

Recommendation: Seth should either finish writing his novel, or find a hobby writing group to join. He would also be a great street team leader for his favorite published author. And maybe the timing will be better sometime down the road for him to return to writing more seriously.

362. Coaching case study: Jump-Around Jenny

Jenny is a prolific writer. She's so prolific, she writes for three publishers, and she writes a different category of fiction for each: contemporary romance for publisher 1, historical erotica for publisher 2, and young adult mysteries for publisher 3. Her agent suggested and Jenny agreed to write under three pen names to keep from confusing her readers. But now she's feeling as if she's on a hamster wheel trying to please three editors. Her deadlines criss-cross and she can't seem to get sales traction in any one category. Plus she has to market and promote three different names to three different audiences through websites and social media. Jenny is exhausted, but she's afraid to pull the plug on any of her publishers.

Assessment: Jenny needs to focus her efforts in one direction, but she doesn't want to make a decision that might be wrong and/or risk upsetting her agent or her editors.

Recommendation: Jenny should conference with her agent and decide which one of the three categories is the most promising, and phase out writing for the other two publishers when the current contracts are fulfilled. Even if the category she chooses to concentrate on suddenly falls out of favor with readers, it can't be worse than her current untenable schedule.

363. Coaching case study: In-a-Rut Rhonda

Rhonda sold her first manuscript to a reputable publisher and over the years, has continued to deliver 1-2 manuscripts a year to her editor. Rhonda is a good-girl author—she always delivers her books on time, and always takes whatever assignments her editors suggests—a holiday book here, a beach read there. Her editor assured Rhonda she would rise above the midlist after she got a few books behind her. Her modest advances grew every few books for a while, but recently, have been cut because sales for the line have suffered. The books she writes now earn less revenue than the books she wrote five years ago. At this point, she has no confidence in being moved out of the midlist; in fact, she's losing ground! Rhonda would like to change tack, but she's heard the industry is so unstable, she's afraid this isn't a good time to switch publishers. And she doesn't want to burn any bridges.

Assessment: Rhonda has happily put her career in her editor's hands, assuming her editor was looking out for her best interests. Her editor is not a mean person, but her editor is looking out for herself, and having a reliable contributor for her line like Rhonda is good for her, so she hasn't gone out of her way to "promote" Rhonda.

Recommendation: Rhonda should tell her editor she wants to be moved out of the midlist with the next contract, and ask what they both need to do to make it happen. If her editor balks, she needs to quietly start looking for a new publishing home because the situation isn't going to improve. But it's up to Rhonda to come up with a great idea to snag the attention of an

STEPHANIE BOND

editor at another publishing house. She has to be proactive if she wants to get ahead—and she has to be willing to take a risk.

412

364. Coaching case study: Bratty Ben

Ben is a veteran writer who's had a nice career any writer would covet. His advances are way above the industry average and his books regularly hit the bestseller lists. But lately he's feeling bored with the books he's writing and is finding it harder and harder to meet his deadlines. He cringes when his editor calls to ask how the book is coming along, and he's toying with writing something completely different than the book he contracted.

Assessment: Ben is being a brat! He has exactly what he asked for and now he wants something else.

Recommendation: Ben needs to put on his big-boy pants. When a writer builds a successful career, he forms a partnership with his readers, his agent, and his publisher who have supported him. He should be honest with his agent and publisher about his desire to move in another direction *on the next contract*. Meanwhile, he should deliver the book his editor bought and his readers are expecting. Being a professional novelist means finding a balance between honoring the creative drive and the demands of the marketplace.

365. Reference books I recommend

Desk reference:
Chicago Manual of Style, University of Chicago Press
Writers Market, Writers Digest

Writing:
Self-Editing for Fiction Writers, Renni Browne and Dave King
Writing the Breakout Novel, Donald Maass
Save the Cat, Blake Snyder (plotting beatsheet)
Elements of Fiction Writing: Beginnings, Middles & Ends, Nancy Kress
Elements of Fiction Writing: Characters & Viewpoint, Orson Scott Card

Motivational:
Writing from the Inside Out: Transforming Your Psychological Blocks to Release the Writer Within, Dennis Palumbo
Manage Your Day-to-Day: Build Your Routine, Find Your Focus & Sharpen Your Creative Mind, 99U
Leap First: Creating Work That Matters, Seth Godin (audiobook)
Fail. Fail Again. Fail Better., Pema Chödrön

Business:
The Naked Truth About Self-Publishing, Tina Folsom, Jana DeLeon, Colleen Gleason, Jane Graves, Debra Holland, Dorien Kelly, Theresa Ragan, Denise Grover Swank, Jasinda Wilder

FINAL PEP TALK

The buzzer is sounding—we did it! Cue the confetti and the balloons!

I hope some portion of this book has resonated with you to get you excited about writing a novel! This is an *amazing* time to be a writer—storytelling is permeating every aspect of entertainment and business. Books are reaching more and more readers all over the world every day, in every language, in every format. If you're willing to invest time and energy into your writing, there are no limits to what you can achieve.

Go, go, go!

A note from the author

Thank you so much for reading YOUR PERSONAL FICTION-WRITING COACH. This book marks a personal and professional milestone for me; it represents twenty years of information from my workshops, articles, blogs, and disconnected bits backed up in my brain. My friends have been bugging me for years to publish a book about writing; I think I had to employ every trick I suggested in this book to actually finish writing it!

On the subject of my advice, please remember these are the methods that work for *me*. But every writer's journey is a singular experience, which is what makes this job so elusive, so frustrating, and so magnificent. No matter where your story takes you, I sincerely wish for you the joy in your writing that my writing has brought to me.

If you enjoyed YOUR PERSONAL FICTION-WRITING COACH and feel inclined to leave an Amazon review, I would appreciate it very much. Writers know better than anyone books live and die by reviews these days. Plus I'd really like to know what you think of the book. Along those lines, I want to hear your success stories! Post to my social media accounts and let me know when you've finished/sold/self-published your novel—and don't forget to mention the title of your book!

Also, although I can't count the times this book has been edited and proofed, I am human, so if you do spot a typo, please email me at **stephanie@stephaniebond.com** to let me know! Thanks again for your time and interest. I wish you nothing but success!

Much love and laughter,

Stephanie Bond

About the author

Stephanie Bond was seven years deep into a corporate career in computer programming and pursuing an MBA at night when an instructor remarked she had a flair for writing and suggested she submit material to academic journals. But Stephanie was more interested in writing fiction—more specifically, romance and mystery novels. After writing in her spare time for two years, she sold her first manuscript; after selling ten additional projects to two publishers, she left her corporate job to write fiction full-time. To-date, Stephanie has more than seventy published novels to her name, including the popular BODY MOVERS humorous mystery series. Stephanie lives in Atlanta. For more information on Stephanie's books, visit **www.stephaniebond.com**.

Made in the USA
Columbia, SC
25 August 2018